PENGUIN

Some Extrao

GW01043888

Charles Mackay
1814–1889

Charles Mackay

Some Extraordinary Popular Delusions

PENGUIN BOOKS — GREAT IDEAS

PENGUIN BOOKS

Published by the Penguin Group
Penguin Books Ltd, 80 Strand, London WC2R 0RL, England
Penguin Group (USA) Inc., 375 Hudson Street, New York, New York 10014, USA
Penguin Group (Canada), 90 Eglinton Avenue East, Suite 700, Toronto, Ontario, Canada M4P 2Y3
(a division of Pearson Penguin Canada Inc.)
Penguin Ireland, 25 St Stephen's Green, Dublin 2, Ireland (a division of Penguin Books Ltd)
Penguin Group (Australia), 250 Camberwell Road, Camberwell, Victoria 3124, Australia
(a division of Pearson Australia Group Pty Ltd)
Penguin Books India Pvt Ltd, 11 Community Centre, Panchsheel Park,
New Delhi – 110 017, India
Penguin Group (NZ), 67 Apollo Drive, Rosedale, North Shore 0632, New Zealand
(a division of Pearson New Zealand Ltd)
Penguin Books (South Africa) (Pty) Ltd, 24 Sturdee Avenue, Rosebank, Johannesburg 2196,
South Africa

Penguin Books Ltd, Registered Offices: 80 Strand, London WC2R 0RL, England

www.penguin.com

Extraordinary Popular Delusions and the Madness of Crowds first published 1841
This selection published in Penguin Books 2010

1

All rights reserved

Set in 11/13 Dante MT Std
Typeset by TexTech International
Printed in England by Clays Ltd, St Ives plc

ISBN: 978-0-141-19292-5

www.greenpenguin.co.uk

Contents

I

Popular Follies of Great Cities

La faridondaine – la faridondon,
Vive la faridondaine!

Beranger

The popular humours of a great city are a never-failing source of amusement to the man whose sympathies are hospitable enough to embrace all his kind, and who, refined though he may be himself, will not sneer at the humble wit or grotesque peculiarities of the boozing mechanic, the squalid beggar, the vicious urchin, and all the motley group of the idle, the reckless, and the imitative that swarm in the alleys and broadways of a metropolis. He who walks through a great city to find subjects for weeping, may, God knows, find plenty at every corner to wring his heart; but let such a man walk on his course, and enjoy his grief alone – we are not of those who would accompany him. The miseries of us poor earthdwellers gain no alleviation from the sympathy of those who merely hunt them out to be pathetic over them. The weeping philosopher too often impairs his eyesight by his woe, and becomes unable from his tears to see the remedies for the evils which he deplores. Thus it will often be found that the man of no tears is the truest philanthropist, as he is the best physician who wears a cheerful face, even in the worst of cases.

So many pens have been employed to point out the miseries, and so many to condemn the crimes and vices, and more serious follies of the multitude, that our's shall not increase the number, at least in this chapter. Our present task shall be less ungracious, and wandering through the busy haunts of great cities, we shall seek only for amusement, and note as we pass a few of the harmless follies and whimsies of the poor.

And, first of all, walk where we will, we cannot help hearing from every side a phrase repeated with delight, and received with laughter, by men with hard hands and dirty faces – by saucy butcher lads and errand-boys – by loose women – by hackney coachmen, cabriolet drivers, and idle fellows who loiter at the corners of streets. Not one utters this phrase without producing a laugh from all within hearing. It seems applicable to every circumstance, and is the universal answer to every question; in short, it is the favourite slang phrase of the day, a phrase that, while its brief season of popularity lasts, throws a dash of fun and frolicsomeness over the existence of squalid poverty and ill-requited labour, and gives them reason to laugh as well as their more fortunate fellows in a higher stage of society.

London is peculiarly fertile in this sort of phrases, which spring up suddenly, no one knows exactly in what spot, and pervade the whole population in a few hours, no one knows how. Many years ago the favourite phrase (for, though but a monosyllable, it was a phrase in itself) was 'Quoz'. This odd word took the fancy of the multitude in an extraordinary degree, and very soon acquired an almost boundless meaning. When vulgar wit wished

2

to mark its incredulity and raise a laugh at the same time, there was no resource so sure as this popular piece of slang. When a man was asked a favour which he did not choose to grant, he marked his sense of the suitor's unparalleled presumption by exclaiming 'Quoz!' When a mischievous urchin wished to annoy a passenger, and create mirth for his chums, he looked him in the face, and cried out 'Quoz!' and the exclamation never failed in its object. When a disputant was desirous of throwing a doubt upon the veracity of his opponent, and getting summarily rid of an argument which he could not overturn, he uttered the word 'Quoz', with a contemptuous curl of his lip and an impatient shrug of his shoulders. The universal monosyllable conveyed all his meaning, and not only told his opponent that he lied, but that he erred egregiously if he thought that anyone was such a nincompoop as to believe him. Every alehouse resounded with 'Quoz'; every street corner was noisy with it, and every wall for miles around was chalked with it.

But, like all other earthly things, 'Quoz' had its season, and passed away as suddenly as it arose, never again to be the pet and the idol of the populace. A new claimant drove it from its place, and held undisputed sway till, in its turn, it was hurled from its pre-eminence, and a successor appointed in its stead

'What a shocking bad hat!' was the phrase that was next in vogue. No sooner had it become universal, than thousands of idle but sharp eyes were on the watch for the passenger whose hat showed any signs, however slight, of ancient service. Immediately the cry arose, and, like the what-whoop of the Indians, was repeated by a hundred discordant throats. He was a wise man who, finding himself under these circumstances 'the observed of all observers', bore his honours meekly. He who showed symptoms of ill-feeling at the imputations cast upon his hat, only brought upon himself redoubled notice. The mob soon perceive whether a man is irritable, and, if of their own class, they love to make sport of him. When such a man, and with such a hat, passed in those days through a crowded neighbourhood, he might think himself fortunate if his annoyances were confined to the shouts and cries of the populace. The obnoxious hat was often snatched from his head, and thrown into the gutter by some practical joker, and then raised, covered with mud, upon the end of a stick, for the admiration of the spectators, who held their sides with laughter, and exclaimed in the pauses of their mirth, 'Oh! what a shocking bad hat!' 'What a shocking bad hat!' Many a nervous, poor man, whose purse could but ill spare the outlay, doubtless purchased a new hat before the time, in order to avoid exposure in this manner.

The origin of this singular saying, which made fun for the metropolis for months, is not involved in the same obscurity as that which shrouds the origin of Quoz and some others. There had been a hotly contested election for the borough of Southwark, and one of the candidates was an eminent hatter. This gentleman, in canvassing the electors, adopted a somewhat professional mode of conciliating their goodwill, and of bribing them without letting them perceive that they were bribed. Whenever he called upon or met a voter whose hat was not of the best material, or, being so, had seen its best days, he invariably said, 'What a shocking bad hat you have got; call at my warehouse, and you shall have a new one!' Upon the day of election this circumstance was remembered, and his opponents made the most of it, by inciting the crowd to keep up an incessant cry of 'What a shocking bad hat!' all the time the honourable candidate was addressing them. From Southwark the phrase spread over all London, and reigned, for a time, the supreme slang of the season.

Hookey Walker, derived from the chorus of a popular ballad, was also high in favour at one time, and served, like its predecessor, Quoz, to answer all questions. In the course of time the latter word alone became the favourite, and was uttered with a peculiar drawl upon the first syllable, and a sharp turn upon the last. If a lively servant girl was importuned for a kiss by a fellow she did not care about, she cocked her little nose, and cried 'Walker!' If a dustman asked his friend for the loan of a shilling, and his friend was either unable or unwilling to accommodate him, the probable answer he would receive was 'Walker!' If a drunken man was reeling along the streets, and a boy pulled his coat-tails, or a man knocked his hat over his eyes to make fun of him, the joke was always accompanied by the same exclamation. This lasted for two or three months, and 'Walker!' walked off the stage, never more to be revived for the entertainment of that or any future generation.

The next phrase was a most preposterous one. Who invented it, how it arose, or where it was first heard, are alike unknown. Nothing about it is certain, but that for months it was the slang par excellence of the Londoners, and afforded them a vast gratification. 'There he goes with his eye out!' or 'There she goes with her eye out!' as the sex of the party alluded to might be, was in the mouth of everybody who knew the town. The sober part of the community were as much puzzled by this unaccountable saying as the vulgar were delighted with it. The wise thought it very foolish, but the many thought it very funny, and the idle amused themselves by chalking it upon walls, or scribbling it upon monuments. But, 'all that's bright must fade', even in slang. The people grew tired of their hobby, and 'There he goes with his eye out!' was heard no more in its accustomed haunts.

Another very odd phrase came into repute in a brief space afterwards, in the form of the impertinent and not universally apposite query, 'Has your mother sold her mangle?' But its popularity was not of that boisterous and cordial kind which ensures a long continuance of favour. What tended to impede its progress was, that it could not be well applied to the older portions of society. It consequently ran but a brief career, and then sank into oblivion. Its successor enjoyed a more extended fame, and laid its foundations so deep, that years and changing fashions have not sufficed to eradicate it. This phrase was 'Flare up!' and it is, even now, a colloquialism in common use. It took its rise in the time of the Reform riots, when Bristol was nearly half burned by the infuriated populace. The flames were said to have flared up in the devoted city. Whether there was anything peculiarly captivating in the sound, or in the idea of these words, is hard to say; but whatever was the reason, it tickled the mob-fancy mightily, and drove all other slang out of the field before it. Nothing was to be heard all over London but 'flare up!' It answered all questions, settled all disputes, was applied to all persons, all things, and all circumstances, and became suddenly the most comprehensive phrase in the English language. The man who had overstepped the bounds of decorum in his speech was said to have flared up; he who had paid visits too repeated to the gin-shop, and got damaged in consequence, had flared up. To put oneself into a passion; to stroll out on a nocturnal frolic, and alarm a neighbourhood, or to create a disturbance in any shape, was to flare up. A lovers' quarrel was a flare up; so was a boxing-match between two blackguards in the streets, and the preachers of sedition and revolution recommended the English nation to flare up, like the French. So great a favourite was the word, that people loved to repeat it for its very sound. They delighted apparently in hearing their own organs articulate it; and labouring men, when none who could respond to the call were within hearing, would often startle the aristocratic echoes of the West by the well-known slang phrase of the East. Even in the dead hours of the night, the ears of those who watched late, or who could not sleep, were saluted with the same sound. The drunkard reeling home showed that he was still a man and a citizen, by calling 'flare up' in the pauses of his hiccough. Drink had deprived him of the power of arranging all other ideas; his intellect was sunk to the level of the brute's; but he clung to humanity by the one last link of the popular cry. While he could vociferate that sound, he had rights as an Englishman, and would not sleep in a gutter, like a dog! Onwards he went, disturbing quiet streets and comfortable people by his whoop, till exhausted nature could support him no more, and he rolled powerless into the road. When, in due time afterwards, the policeman stumbled upon him as he lay, that guardian of the peace turned the full light of his lantern on his face, and exclaimed, 'Here's a poor devil who's been flaring up!' Then came the stretcher, on which the victim of deep potations was carried to the watchhouse, and pitched into a dirty cell, among a score of wretches about as far gone as himself, who saluted their new comrade by a loud, long shout of 'flare up!'

So universal was this phrase, and so enduring seemed its popularity, that a speculator, who knew not the evanescence of slang, established a weekly newspaper under its name. But he was like the man who built his house upon the sand; his foundation gave way under him, and the phrase and the newspaper were washed into the mighty sea of the things that were. The people grew at last weary of the monotony, and 'flare up' became vulgar even among them. Gradually it was left to little boys who did not know the world, and in process of time sank altogether into neglect. It is now heard no more as a piece of popular slang; but the words are still used to signify any sudden outburst either of fire, disturbance, or ill-nature.

The next phrase that enjoyed the favour of the million was less concise, and seems to have been originally aimed against precocious youths who gave themselves the airs of manhood before their time. 'Does your mother know you're out?' was the provoking query addressed to young men of more than reasonable swagger, who smoked cigars in the streets, and wore false whiskers to look irresistible. We have seen many a conceited fellow who could not suffer a woman to pass him without staring her out of countenance, reduced at once into his natural insignificance by the mere utterance of this phrase. Apprentice lads and shopmen in their Sunday clothes held the words in abhorrence, and looked fierce when they were applied to them. Altogether the phrase had a very salutary effect, and in a thousand instances showed young Vanity, that it was not half so pretty and engaging as it thought itself. What rendered it so provoking was the doubt it implied as to the capability of self-guidance possessed by the individual to whom it was addressed. 'Does your mother know you're out?' was a query of mock concern and solicitude, implying regret and concern that one so young and inexperienced in the ways of a great city should be allowed to wander abroad without the guidance of a parent. Hence the great wrath of those who verged on manhood, but had not reached it, whenever they were made the subject of it. Even older heads did not like it; and the heir of a ducal house, and inheritor of a warrior's name, to whom they were applied by a cabriolet driver, who was ignorant of his rank, was so indignant at the affront, that he summoned the offender before the magisterial bench. The fellow had wished to impose upon his Lordship by asking double the fare he was entitled to, and when his Lordship resisted the demand, he was insultingly asked 'if his mother knew he was out?' All the drivers on the stand joined in the query, and his Lordship was fain to escape their laughter by walking away with as much haste as his dignity would allow. The man pleaded ignorance that his customer was a Lord, but offended justice fined him for his mistake.

When this phrase had numbered its appointed days, it died away, like its predecessors, and 'Who are you?' reigned in its stead. This new favourite, like a mushroom, seems to have sprung up in a night, or, like a frog in Cheapside, to have come down in a sudden shower. One day it was unheard, unknown, uninvented; the next it pervaded London; every alley resounded with it; every highway was musical with it,

> And street to street, and lane to lane flung back
> The one unvarying cry.

The phrase was uttered quickly, and with a sharp sound upon the first and last words, leaving the middle one little more than an aspiration. Like all its compeers which had been extensively popular, it was applicable to almost every variety of circumstance. The lovers of a plain answer to a plain question did not like it at all. Insolence made use of it to give offence; ignorance, to avoid exposing itself; and waggery, to create laughter. Every new comer into an alehouse tap-room was asked unceremoniously, 'Who are you?' and if he looked foolish, scratched his head, and did not know what to reply, shouts of boisterous merriment resounded on every side. An authoritative disputant was not infrequently put down, and presumption of every kind checked by the same query. When its popularity was at its height, a gentleman, feeling the hand of a thief in his pocket, turned suddenly round, and caught him in the act, exclaiming, 'Who are you?' The mob which gathered round applauded to the very echo, and thought it the most capital joke they had ever heard – the very acme of wit – the very essence of humour. Another circumstance, of a similar kind, gave an additional fillip to the phrase, and infused new life and vigour into it, just as it was dying away. The scene occurred in the chief criminal court of the kingdom. A prisoner stood at the bar; the offence with which he had been charged was clearly proved against him; his counsel had been heard, not in his defence, but in extenuation, insisting upon his previous good life and character, as reasons for the lenity of the court. 'And where are your witnesses?' enquired the learned judge who presided. 'Please you, my Lord, I knows the prisoner at the bar, and a more honester feller never breathed,' said a rough voice in the gallery. The officers of the court looked aghast, and the strangers tittered with ill-suppressed laughter. 'Who are you?' said the Judge, looking suddenly up, but with imperturbable gravity. The court was convulsed; the titter broke out into a laugh, and it was several minutes before silence and decorum could be restored. When the Ushers recovered their self-possession, they made diligent search for the profane transgressor; but he was not to be found. Nobody knew him; nobody had seen him. After a while the business of the court again proceeded. The next prisoner brought up for trial augured favourably of his prospects when he learned that the solemn lips of the representative of justice had uttered the popular phrase as if he felt and appreciated it. There was no fear that such a judge would use undue severity; his heart was with the people; he understood their language and their manners, and would make allowances for the temptations which drove them into crime. So thought many of the prisoners, if we may infer it from the fact, that the learned judge suddenly acquired an immense increase of popularity. The praise of his wit was in every mouth, and 'Who are you?' renewed its lease, and remained in possession of public favour for another term in consequence.

But it must not be supposed that there were no *interregna* between the dominion of one slang phrase and another. They did not arise in one long line of unbroken succession, but shared with song the possession of popular favour. Thus, when the people were in the mood for music, slang advanced its claims to no purpose, and, when they were inclined for slang, the sweet voice of music wooed them in vain. About twenty years ago London resounded with one chorus, with the love of which everybody seemed to be smitten. Girls and boys, young men and old, maidens and wives, and widows, were all alike musical. There was an absolute mania for singing, and the worst of it was, that, like good Father Philip, in the romance of *The Monastery*, they seemed utterly unable to change their tune. 'Cherry ripe!' 'Cherry ripe!' was the universal cry of all the idle in the town. Every unmelodious voice gave utterance to it; every crazy fiddle, every cracked flute, every wheezy pipe, every street organ was heard in the same strain, until studious and quiet men stopped their ears in desperation, or fled miles away into the fields or woodlands, to be at peace. This plague lasted for a twelvemonth, until the very name of cherries became an abomination in the land. At last the excitement wore itself away, and the tide of favour set in a new direction. Whether it was another song or a slang phrase, is difficult to determine at this distance of time; but certain it is, that very shortly afterwards, people went mad upon a dramatic subject, and nothing was to be heard of but 'Tom and Jerry'. Verbal wit had amused the multitude long enough, and they became more practical in their recreation. Every youth on the town was seized with the fierce desire of distinguishing himself, by knocking down the 'charlies', being locked up all night in a watchhouse, or kicking up a row among loose women and blackguard men in the low dens of St Giles's. Imitative boys vied with their elders in similar exploits, until this unworthy passion, for such it was, had lasted, like other follies, its appointed time, and the town became merry after another fashion. It was next thought the height of vulgar wit to answer all questions by placing the point of the thumb upon the tip of the nose, and twirling the fingers in the air. If one man wished to insult or annoy another, he had only to make use of this cabalistic sign in his face, and his object was accomplished. At every street corner where a group was assembled, the spectator who was curious enough to observe their movements, would be sure to see the fingers of some of them at their noses, either as a mark of incredulity, surprise, refusal, or mockery, before he had watched two minutes. There is some remnant of this absurd custom to be seen to this day; but it is thought low, even among the vulgar.

About sixteen years ago, London became again most preposterously musical. The *vox populi* wore itself hoarse by singing the praises of 'The Sea, the Sea!' If a stranger (and a philosopher) had walked through London, and listened to the universal chorus, he might have constructed a very pretty theory upon the love of the English for the sea-service, and our acknowledged superiority over all other nations upon that element. 'No wonder,' he might have said, 'that this people is invincible upon the ocean. The love of it mixes with their daily thoughts: they celebrate it even in the market-place: their street-minstrels excite charity by it; and high and low, young and old, male and female, chant '*Io poeans*' in its praise. Love is not honoured in the national songs of this warlike race – Bacchus is no god to them; they are men of sterner mould, and think only of "the Sea, the Sea!" and the means of conquering upon it.'

Such would, doubtless, have been his impression if he had taken the evidence only of his ears. Alas! in those days for the refined ears that *were* musical! great was their torture when discord, with its thousand diversities of tone, struck up this appalling anthem – there was no escape from it. The migratory minstrels of Savoy caught the strain, and pealed it down the long vistas of quiet streets, till their innermost and snuggest apartments re-echoed with the sound. Men were obliged to endure this crying evil for full six months, wearied to desperation, and made seasick on the dry land.

Several other songs sprang up in due succession afterwards, but none of them, with the exception of one, entitled 'All round my Hat', enjoyed any extraordinary share of favour, until an American actor introduced a vile song called 'Jim Crow'. The singer sang his verses in appropriate costume, with grotesque gesticulations, and a sudden whirl of his body at the close of each verse. It took the taste of the town immediately, and for months the ears of orderly people were stunned by the senseless chorus:

> Turn about and wheel about,
>   And do just so –
> Turn about and wheel about,
>   And jump, Jim Crow!

Street-minstrels blackened their faces in order to give proper effect to the verses; and fatherless urchins, who had to choose between thieving and singing for their livelihood, took the latter course, as likely to be the more profitable, as long as the public taste remained in that direction. The uncouth dance, its accompaniment, might be seen in its full perfection on market nights in any great thoroughfare; and the words of the song might be heard, piercing above all the din and buzz of the ever-moving multitude. He, the calm observer, who, during the heyday popularity of this doggerel,

>   Sat beside the public way,
>   Thick strewn with summer dust, and saw the stream
>   Of people there was hurrying to and fro,
>   Numerous as gnats upon the evening gleam,

might have exclaimed with Shelley, whose fine lines we quote, that

>   The million, with fierce song and maniac dance,
>   Did rage around.

The philosophic theorist we have already supposed soliloquising upon the English character, and forming his opinion of it from their exceeding love for a sea-song, might, if he had again dropped suddenly into London, have formed another very plausible theory to account for our unremitting efforts for the abolition of the Slave Trade. 'Benevolent people!' he might have said, 'how unbounded are your sympathies! Your unhappy brethren of Africa, differing from you only in the colour of their skins, are so dear to you, and you begrudge so little the twenty millions you have paid on their behalf, that you love to have a memento of them continually in your sight. Jim Crow is the representative of that injured race, and as such is the idol of your populace! See how they all sing his praises! – how they imitate his peculiarities! – how they repeat his name in their moments of leisure and relaxation! They even carve images of him to adorn their hearths, that his cause and his sufferings may never be forgotten! Oh, philanthropic England! – oh, vanguard of civilisation!'

Such are a few of the peculiarities of the London multitude, when no riot, no execution, no murder, no balloon, disturbs the even current of their thoughts. These are the whimseys of the mass – the harmless follies by which they unconsciously endeavour to lighten the load of care which presses upon their existence. The wise man, even though he smile at them, will not altogether withhold his sympathy, and will say, 'Let them enjoy their slang phrases and their choruses if they will; and if they cannot be happy, at least let them be merry.' To the Englishman, as well as to the Frenchman of whom Beranger sings, there may be some comfort in so small a thing as a song, and we may, own with him that

Au peuple attristé
Ce qui rendra la gaîté,

C'est la GAUDRIOLE!
O gué!
C'est la GAUDRIOLE!'

2

The South-Sea Bubble

At length corruption, like a general flood,
Did deluge all, and avarice creeping on,
Spread, like a low-born mist, and hid the sun.
Statesmen and patriots plied alike the stocks,
Peeress and butler shared alike the box;
And judges jobbed, and bishops bit the town,
And mighty dukes packed cards for half a crown:
Britain was sunk in lucre's sordid charms.

Pope

The South-Sea Company was originated by the celebrated Harley, Earl of Oxford, in the year 1711, with the view of restoring public credit, which had suffered by the dismissal of the Whig ministry, and of providing for the discharge of the army and navy debentures, and other parts of the floating debt, amounting to nearly ten millions sterling. A company of merchants, at that time without a name, took this debt upon themselves, and the government agreed to secure them, for a certain period, the interest of six per cent. To provide for this interest, amounting to £600,000 per annum, the duties upon wines, vinegar, India goods, wrought silks, tobacco, whale-fins, and some other articles, were rendered permanent. The monopoly of the trade to the South Seas was granted, and the company, being incorporated by Act of Parliament, assumed the title by which it has ever since been known. The minister took great credit to himself for his share in this transaction, and the scheme was always called by his flatterers 'the Earl of Oxford's masterpiece'.

Even at this early period of its history, the most visionary ideas were formed by the company and the public of the immense riches of the western coast of South America. Everybody had heard of the gold and silver mines of Peru and Mexico; everyone believed them to be inexhaustible, and that it was only necessary to send the manufactures of England to the coast, to be repaid a hundredfold in gold and silver ingots by the natives. A report, industriously spread, that Spain was willing to concede four ports, on the coasts of Chile and Peru for the purposes of traffic, increased the general confidence, and for many years the South-Sea Company's stock was in high favour.

Philip V of Spain, however, never had any intention of admitting the English to a free trade in the ports of Spanish America. Negotiations were set on foot, but their only result was the *assiento* contract, or the privilege of supplying the colonies with Negroes for thirty years, and of sending once a year a vessel, limited both as to tonnage and value of cargo, to trade with Mexico, Peru, or Chile. The latter permission was only granted upon the hard condition, that the King of Spain should enjoy one-fourth of the profits, and a tax of five per cent on the remainder. This was a great disappointment to the Earl of Oxford and his party, who were reminded much oftener than they found agreeable of the '*Parturiunt montes, nascitur ridiculus mus'*. But the public confidence in the South-Sea Company was not shaken. The Earl of Oxford declared that Spain would permit two ships, in addition to the annual ship, to carry out merchandise during the first year; and a list was published, in which all the ports and harbours of these coasts were pompously set forth as open to the trade of Great Britain. The first voyage of the annual ship was not made till the year 1717, and in the following year the trade was suppressed by the rupture with Spain.

The king's speech, at the opening of the session of 1717, made pointed allusion to the state of public credit, and recommended that proper measures should be taken to reduce the national debt. The two great monetary corporations, the South-Sea Company and the Bank of England, made proposals to parliament on the 20th of May ensuing. The South-Sea Company prayed that their capital stock of ten millions might be increased to twelve, by subscription or otherwise, and offered to accept five per cent instead of six upon the whole amount. The bank made proposals equally advantageous. The house debated for some time, and finally three acts were passed, called the South-Sea Act, the Bank Act, and the General Fund Act. By the first, the proposals of the South-Sea Company were accepted, and that body held itself ready to advance the sum of two millions towards discharging the principal and interest of the debt due by the state for the four lottery funds of the ninth and tenth years of Queen Anne. By the second act, the bank received a lower rate of interest for the sum of £1,775,027 15s. due to it by the state, and agreed to deliver up to be cancelled as many exchequer bills as amounted to two millions sterling, and to accept of an annuity of one hundred thousand pounds, being after the rate of five per cent, the whole redeemable at one year's notice. They were further required to be ready to advance, in case of need, a sum not exceeding £2,500,000 upon the same terms of five per cent interest, redeemable by parliament. The General Fund Act recited the various deficiencies, which were to be made good by the aids derived from the foregoing sources.

The name of the South-Sea Company was thus continually before the public. Though their trade with the South American States produced little or no augmentation of their revenues, they continued to flourish as a monetary corporation. Their stock was in high request, and the directors, buoyed up with success, began to think of new means for extending their influence. The Mississippi scheme of John Law, which so dazzled and captivated the French people, inspired them with an idea that they could carry on the same game in England. The anticipated failure of his plans did not divert them from their intention. Wise in their own conceit, they imagined they could avoid his faults, carry on their schemes for ever, and stretch the cord of credit to its extremest tension, without causing it to snap asunder.

It was while Law's plan was at its greatest height of popularity, while people were crowding in thousands to the Rue Quincampoix, and ruining themselves with frantic eagerness, that the South-Sea directors laid before parliament their famous plan for paying off the national debt. Visions of boundless wealth floated before the fascinated eyes of the people in the two most celebrated countries of Europe. The English commenced their career of extravagance somewhat later than the French; but as soon as the delirium seized them, they were determined not to be outdone. Upon the 22nd of January, 1720, the House of Commons resolved itself into a committee of the whole house, to take into consideration that part of the king's speech at the opening of the session which related to the public debts, and the proposal of the South-Sea Company towards the redemption and sinking of the same. The proposal set forth at great length, and under several heads, the debts of the state, amounting to £30,981,712 which the company were anxious to take upon themselves, upon consideration of five per cent per annum, secured to them until Midsummer 1727; after which time, the whole was to become redeemable at the pleasure of the legislature, and the interest to be reduced to four per cent. The proposal was received with great favour; but the Bank of England had many friends in the House of Commons, who were desirous that that body should share in the advantages that were likely to accrue. On behalf of this corporation it was represented, that they had performed great and eminent services to the state in the most difficult times, and deserved, at least, that if any advantage was to be made by public bargains of this nature, they should be preferred before a company that had never done anything for the nation. The further consideration of the matter was accordingly postponed for five days. In the mean time, a plan was drawn up by the governors of the bank. The South-Sea Company, afraid that the bank might offer still more advantageous terms to the government than themselves, reconsidered their former proposal, and made some alterations in it, which they hoped would render it more acceptable. The principal change was a stipulation that the government might redeem these debts at the expiration of four years, instead of seven, as at first suggested. The bank resolved not to be outbidden in this singular auction, and the governors also reconsidered their first proposal, and sent in a new one.

Thus, each corporation having made two proposals, the house began to deliberate. Mr Robert Walpole was the chief speaker in favour of the bank, and Mr Aislabie, the Chancellor of the Exchequer, the principal advocate on behalf of the South-Sea Company. It was resolved, on the 2nd of February, that the proposals of the latter were most advantageous to the country. They were accordingly received, and leave was given to bring in a bill to that effect.

Exchange Alley was in a fever of excitement. The company's stock, which had been at a hundred and thirty the previous day, gradually rose to three hundred, and continued to rise with the most astonishing rapidity during the whole time that the bill in its several stages was under discussion. Mr Walpole was almost the only statesman in the house who spoke out boldly against it. He warned them, in eloquent and solemn language, of the evils that would ensue. It countenanced, he said, 'the dangerous practice of stock-jobbing, and would divert the genius of the nation from trade and industry. It would hold out a dangerous lure to decoy the unwary to their ruin, by making them part with the earnings of their labour for a prospect of imaginary wealth. The great principle of the project was an evil of first-rate magnitude; it was to raise artificially the value of the stock, by exciting and keeping up a general infatuation, and by promising dividends out of funds which could never be adequate to the purpose.' In a prophetic spirit he added, that if the plan succeeded, the directors would become masters of the government, form a new and absolute aristocracy in the kingdom, and control the resolutions of the legislature. If it failed, which he was convinced it would, the result would bring general discontent and ruin upon the country. Such would be the delusion, that when the evil day came, as come it would, the people would start up, as from a dream, and ask themselves if these things could have been true. All his eloquence was in vain. He was looked upon as a false prophet, or compared to the hoarse raven, croaking omens of evil. His friends, however, compared him to Cassandra, predicting evils which would only be believed when they came home to men's hearths, and stared them in the face at their own boards. Although, in former times, the house had listened with the utmost attention to every word that fell from his lips, the benches became deserted when it was known that he would speak on the South-Sea question.

The bill was two months in its progress through the House of Commons. During this time every exertion was made by the directors and their friends, and more especially by the chairman, the noted Sir John Blunt, to raise the price of the stock. The most extravagant rumours were in circulation. Treaties between England and Spain were spoken of, whereby the latter was to grant a free trade to all her colonies; and the rich produce of the mines of Potosi-la-Paz was to be brought to England until silver should become almost as plentiful as iron. For cotton and woollen goods, with which we could supply them in abundance, the dwellers in Mexico were to empty their golden mines. The company of merchants trading to the South Seas would be the richest the world ever saw, and every hundred pounds invested in it would produce hundreds per annum to the stockholder. At last the stock was raised by these means to near four hundred; but, after fluctuating a good deal, settled at three hundred and thirty, at which price it remained when the bill passed the Commons by a majority of 172 against 55.

In the House of Lords the bill was hurried through all its stages with unexampled rapidity. On the 4th of April it was read a first time; on the 5th, it was read a second time; on the 6th, it was committed; and on the 7th, was read a third time and passed.

Several peers spoke warmly against the scheme; but their warnings fell upon dull, cold ears. A speculating frenzy had seized them as well as the plebeians. Lord North and Grey said the bill was unjust in its nature, and might prove fatal in its consequences, being calculated to enrich the few and impoverish the many. The Duke of Wharton followed; but, as he only retailed at second-hand the arguments so eloquently stated by Walpole in the Lower House, he was not listened to with even the same attention that had been bestowed upon Lord North and Grey. Earl Cowper followed on the same side, and compared the bill to the famous horse of the siege of Troy. Like that, it was ushered in and received with great pomp and acclamations of joy, but bore within it treachery and destruction. The Earl of Sunderland endeavoured to answer all objections; and on the question being put, there appeared only seventeen peers against, and eighty-three in favour of the project. The very same day on which it passed the Lords, it received the Royal assent, and became the law of the land.

It seemed at that time as if the whole nation had turned stock-jobbers. Exchange Alley was every day blocked up by crowds, and Cornhill was impassable for the number of carriages. Everybody came to purchase stock. 'Every fool aspired to be a knave.' In the words of a ballad, published at the time, and sung about the streets,

> Then stars and garters did appear
>   Among the meaner rabble;
> To buy and sell, to see and hear
>   The Jews and Gentiles squabble.
>
> The greatest ladies thither came,
>   And plied in chariots daily,
> Or pawned their jewels for a sum

The inordinate thirst of gain that had afflicted all ranks of society was not to be slaked even in the South Sea. Other schemes, of the most extravagant kind, were started. The share-lists were speedily filled up, and an enormous traffic carried on in shares, while, of course, every means were resorted to to raise them to an artificial value in the market.

Contrary to all expectation, South-Sea stock fell when the bill received the royal assent. On the 7th of April the shares were quoted at three hundred and ten, and on the following day at two hundred and ninety. Already the directors had tasted the profits of their scheme, and it was not likely that they should quietly allow the stock to find its natural level, without an effort to raise it. Immediately their busy emissaries were set to work. Every person interested in the success of the project endeavoured to draw a knot of listeners around him, to whom he expatiated on the treasures of the South American seas. Exchange Alley was crowded with attentive groups. One rumour alone, asserted with the utmost confidence, had an immediate effect upon the stock. It was said that Earl Stanhope had received overtures in France from the Spanish Government to exchange Gibraltar and Port Mahon for some places on the coast of Peru, for the security and enlargement of the trade in the South Seas. Instead of one annual ship trading to those ports, and allowing the king of Spain twenty-five per cent out of the profits, the company might build and charter as many ships as they pleased, and pay no percentage whatever to any foreign potentate. 'Visions of ingots danced before their eyes', and stock rose rapidly. On the 12th of April, five days after the bill had become law, the directors opened their books for a subscription of a million, at the rate of £300 for every £100 capital. Such was the concourse of persons of all ranks, that this first subscription was found to amount to above two millions of original stock. It was to be paid at five payments, of £60 each for every £100. In a few days the stock advanced to three hundred and forty, and the subscriptions were sold for double the price of the first payment. To raise the stock still higher, it was declared, in a general court of directors, on the 21st of April, that the midsummer dividend should be ten per cent, and that all subscriptions should be entitled to the same. These resolutions answering the end designed, the directors, to improve the infatuation of the monied men, opened their books for a second subscription of a million, at four hundred per cent. Such was the frantic eagerness of people of every class to speculate in these funds, that in the course of a few hours no less than a million and a half was subscribed at that rate.

In the mean time, innumerable joint-stock companies started up everywhere. They soon received the name of Bubbles, the most appropriate that imagination could devise. The populace are often most happy in the nicknames they employ. None could be more apt than that of Bubbles. Some of them lasted for a week, or a fortnight, and were no more heard of, while others could not even live out that short span of existence. Every evening produced new schemes, and every morning new projects. The highest of the aristocracy were as eager in this hot pursuit of gain as the most plodding jobber in Cornhill. The Prince of Wales became governor of one company, and is said to have cleared £40,000 by his speculations. The Duke of Bridgewater started a scheme for the improvement of London and Westminster, and the Duke of Chandos another. There were nearly a hundred different projects, each more extravagant and deceptive than the other. To use the words of the *Political State*, they were 'set on foot and promoted by crafty knaves, then pursued by multitudes of covetous fools, and at last appeared to be, in effect, what their vulgar appellation denoted them to be – bubbles and mere cheats'. It was computed that near one million and a half sterling was won and lost by these unwarrantable practices, to the impoverishment of many a fool, and the enriching of many a rogue.

Some of these schemes were plausible enough, and, had they been undertaken at a time when the public mind was unexcited, might have been pursued with advantage to all concerned. But they were established merely with the view of raising the shares in the market. The projectors took the first opportunity of a rise to sell out, and next morning the scheme was at an end. Maitland, in his *History of London*, gravely informs us, that one of the projects which received great encouragement, was for the establishment of a company 'to make deal boards out of sawdust'. This is no doubt intended as a joke; but there is abundance of evidence to show that dozens of schemes, hardly a whit more reasonable, lived their little day, ruining hundreds ere they fell. One of them was for a wheel for perpetual motion – capital, one million; another was 'for encouraging the breed of horses in England, and improving of glebe and church lands, and repairing and rebuilding parsonage and vicarage houses'. Why the clergy, who were so mainly interested in the latter clause, should have taken so much interest in the first, is only to be explained on the supposition that the scheme was projected by a knot of the foxhunting parsons, once so common in England. The shares of this company were rapidly subscribed for. But the most absurd and preposterous of all, and which showed, more completely than any other, the utter madness of the people, was one started by an unknown adventurer, entitled 'A company for carrying on an undertaking of great advantage, but nobody to know what it is'. Were not the fact stated by scores of credible witnesses, it would be impossible to believe that any person could have been duped by such a project. The man of genius who essayed this bold and successful inroad upon public credulity, merely stated in his prospectus that the required capital was half a million, in five thousand shares of £100 each, deposit £2 per share. Each subscriber, paying his deposit, would be entitled to £100 per annum per share. How this immense profit was to be obtained, he did not condescend to inform them at that time, but promised that in a month full particulars should be duly announced, and a call made for the remaining £98 of the subscription. Next morning, at nine o'clock, this great man opened an office in Cornhill. Crowds of people beset his door, and when he shut up at three o'clock, he found that no less than one thousand shares had been subscribed for, and the deposits paid. He was thus, in five hours, the winner of £2,000. He was philosopher enough to be contented with his venture, and set off the same evening for the Continent. He was never heard of again.

Well might Swift exclaim, comparing Change Alley to a gulf in the South Sea:

> Subscribers here by thousands float,
>   And jostle one another down,
> Each paddling in his leaky boat,
>   And here they fish for gold, and drown.
>
> Now buried in the depths below,
>   Now mounted up to heaven again,
> They reel and stagger to and fro,
>   At their wit's end, like drunken men.

> Meantime, secure on Garraway cliffs,
> A savage race, by shipwrecks fed,
> Lie waiting for the foundered skiffs,
> And strip the bodies of the dead.

Another fraud that was very successful was that of the 'Globe Permits', as they were called. They were nothing more than square pieces of playing-cards, on which was the impression of a seal, in wax, bearing the sign of the Globe Tavern, in the neighbourhood of Exchange Alley, with the inscription of 'Sail-Cloth Permits'. The possessors enjoyed no other advantage from them than permission to subscribe at some future time to a new sail-cloth manufactory, projected by one who was then known to be a man of fortune, but who was afterwards involved in the peculation and punishment of the South-Sea directors. These permits sold for as much as sixty guineas in the Alley.

Persons of distinction, of both sexes, were deeply engaged in all these bubbles; those of the male sex going to taverns and coffee-houses to meet their brokers, and the ladies resorting for the same purpose to the shops of milliners and haberdashers. But it did not follow that all these people believed in the feasibility of the schemes to which they subscribed; it was enough for their purpose that their shares would, by stock-jobbing arts, be soon raised to a premium, when they got rid of them with all expedition to the really credulous. So great was the confusion of the crowd in the alley, that shares in the same bubble were known to have been sold at the same instant ten per cent higher at one end of the alley than at the

other. Sensible men beheld the extraordinary infatuation
of the people with sorrow and alarm. There were some
both in and out of parliament who foresaw clearly the
ruin that was impending. Mr Walpole did not cease his
gloomy forebodings. His fears were shared by all the
thinking few, and impressed most forcibly upon the government. On the 11th of June, the day the parliament
rose, the king published a proclamation, declaring that
all these unlawful projects should be deemed public
nuisances, and prosecuted accordingly, and forbidding any
broker, under a penalty of five hundred pounds, from buying or selling any shares in them. Notwithstanding this
proclamation, roguish speculators still carried them on,
and the deluded people still encouraged them. On the
12th of July, an order of the Lords Justices assembled in
privy council was published, dismissing all the petitions
that had been presented for patents and charters, and dis-
solving all the bubble companies. The following copy of
their lordships' order, containing a list of all these nefari-
ous projects, will not be deemed uninteresting at the
present day, when there is but too much tendency in the
public mind to indulge in similar practices:

*At the Council Chamber, Whitehall, the 12th day of July, 1720.
Present, their Excellencies the Lords Justices in Council.*

Their Excellencies, the Lords Justices, in council, taking
into consideration the many inconveniences arising to
the public from several projects set on foot for raising of
joint-stock for various purposes, and that a great many
of his Majesty's subjects have been drawn in to part with

their money on pretence of assurances that their petitions for patents and charters, to enable them to carry on the same, would be granted: to prevent such impositions, their excellencies this day ordered the said several petitions, together with such reports from the Board of Trade, and from his majesty's attorney and solicitor-general, as had been obtained thereon, to be laid before them; and after mature consideration thereof, were pleased, by advice of his majesty's privy council, to order that the said petitions be dismissed, which are as follow:

1. Petition of several persons, praying letters patent for carrying on a fishing trade, by the name of the Grand Fishery of Great Britain.

2. Petition of the Company of the Royal Fishery of England, praying letters patent for such further powers as will effectually contribute to carry on the said fishery.

3. Petition of George James, on behalf of himself and divers persons of distinction concerned in a national fishery, praying letters patent of incorporation to enable them to carry on the same.

4. Petition of several merchants, traders, and others, whose names are thereunto subscribed, praying to be incorporated for reviving and carrying on a whale fishery to Greenland and elsewhere.

5. Petition of Sir John Lambert, and others thereto subscribing, on behalf of themselves and a great number of merchants, praying to be incorporated for carrying on a Greenland trade, and particularly a whale fishery in Davis's Straits.

6. Another petition for a Greenland trade.

7. Petition of several merchants, gentlemen, and citizens, praying to be incorporated for buying and building of ships to let or freight.

8. Petition of Samuel Antrim and others, praying for letters patent for sowing hemp and flax.

9. Petition of several merchants, masters of ships, sail-makers, and manufacturers of sail-cloth, praying a charter of incorporation, to enable them to carry on and promote the said manufactory by a joint-stock.

10. Petition of Thomas Boyd, and several hundred merchants, owners and masters of ships, sail-makers, weavers, and other traders, praying a charter of incorporation, empowering them to borrow money for purchasing lands, in order to the manufacturing sail-cloth and fine Holland.

11. Petition on behalf of several persons interested in a patent granted by the late King William and Queen Mary, for the making of linen and sail-cloth, praying that no charter may be granted to any persons whatsoever for making sail-cloth, but that the privilege now enjoyed by them may be confirmed, and likewise an additional power to carry on the cotton and cotton-silk manufactures.

12. Petition of several citizens, merchants, and traders in London, and others, subscribers to a British stock for a general insurance from fire in any part of England, praying to be incorporated for carrying on the said undertaking.

13. Petition of several of his majesty's loyal subjects of the city of London and other parts of Great Britain, praying to be incorporated for carrying on a general insurance from losses by fire within the kingdom of England.

14. Petition of Thomas Burges, and others his majesty's subjects thereto subscribing, in behalf of themselves and others, subscribers to a fund of £1,200,000 for carrying on a trade to his majesty's German dominions, praying to be incorporated, by the name of the Harburg Company.

15. Petition of Edward Jones, a dealer in timber, on behalf of himself and others, praying to be incorporated for the importation of timber from Germany.

16. Petition of several merchants of London, praying a charter of incorporation for carrying on a salt-work.

17. Petition of Captain Macphedris of London, merchant, on behalf of himself and several merchants, clothiers, hatters, dyers, and other traders, praying a charter of incorporation empowering them to raise a sufficient sum of money to purchase lands for planting and rearing a wood called madder, for the use of dyers.

18. Petition of Joseph Galendo of London, snuffmaker, praying a patent for his invention to prepare and cure Virginia tobacco for snuff in Virginia, and making it into the same in all his majesty's dominions.

LIST OF BUBBLES

The following Bubble Companies were by the same order declared to be illegal, and abolished accordingly:

1. For the importation of Swedish iron.

2. For supplying London with sea-coal. Capital, three millions.

3. For building and rebuilding houses throughout all England. Capital, three millions.

4. For making of muslin.

5. For carrying on and improving British alum-works.

6. For effectually settling the island of Blanco and Sal Targatus.

7. For supplying the town of Deal with fresh water.

8. For the importation of Flanders lace.

9. For improvement in lands of Great Britain. Capital, four millions.

10. For encouraging the breed of horses in England, and improving the glebe and church lands, and for repairing and rebuilding parsonage and vicarage houses.

11. For making of iron and steel in Great Britain.

12. For improving the land in the county of Flint. Capital, one million.

13. For purchasing lands to build on. Capital, two millions.

14. For trading in hair.

15. For erecting salt-works in holy Island. Capital, two millions.

16. For buying and selling estates, and lending money on mortgage.

17. For carrying on an undertaking of great advantage, but nobody to know what it is.

18. For paving the streets of London. Capital, two millions.

19. For furnishing funerals to any part of Great Britain.

20. For buying and selling lands and lending money at interest. Capital, five millions.

21. For carrying on the Royal Fishery of Great Britain. Capital, ten millions.

22. For assuring of seamen's wages.

23. For erecting loan-offices for the assistance and encouragement of the industrious. Capital, two millions.

24. For purchasing and improving leasable lands. Capital, four millions.

25. For importing pitch and tar, and other naval stores, from North Britain and America.

26. For the clothing, felt, and pantile trade.

27. For purchasing and improving a manor and royalty in Essex.

28. For insuring of horses. Capital, two millions.

29. For exporting the woollen manufacture, and importing copper, brass, and iron. Capital, four millions.

30. For a grand dispensary. Capital, three millions.

31. For erecting mills and purchasing lead mines. Capital, two millions.

32. For improving the art of making soap.

33. For a settlement on the island of Santa Cruz.

34. For sinking pits and smelting lead ore in Derbyshire.

35. For making glass bottles and other glass.

36. For a wheel for perpetual motion. Capital, one million.

37. For improving of gardens.

38. For insuring and increasing children's fortunes.

39. For entering and loading goods at the Custom-house, and for negotiating business for merchants.

40. For carrying on a woollen manufacture in the north of England.

41. For importing walnut trees from Virginia. Capital, two millions.

42. For making Manchester stuffs of thread and cotton.

43. For making Joppa and Castile soap.

44. For improving the wrought-iron and steel manufactures of this kingdom. Capital, four millions.

45. For dealing in lace, hollands, cambrics, lawns, &c. Capital, two millions.

46. For trading in and improving certain commodities of the produce of this kingdom, &c. Capital, three millions.

47. For supplying the London markets with cattle.

48. For making looking-glasses, coach glasses, &c. Capital, two millions.

49. For working the tin and lead mines in Cornwall and Derbyshire.

50. For making rape-oil.

51. For importing beaver fur. Capital, two millions.

52. For making pasteboard and packing-paper.

53. For importing of oils and other materials used in the woollen manufacture.

54. For improving and increasing the silk manufactures.

55. For lending money on stock, annuities, tallies, &c.

56. For paying pensions to widows and others, at a small discount. Capital, two millions.

57. For improving malt liquors. Capital, four millions.

58. For a grand American fishery.

59. For purchasing and improving the fenny lands in Lincolnshire. Capital, two millions.

60. For improving the paper manufacture of Great Britain.

61. The Bottomry Company.

62. For drying malt by hot air.

63. For carrying on a trade in the river Oronooko.

64. For the more effectual making of baize, in Colchester and other parts of Great Britain.

65. For buying of naval stores, supplying the victualling, and paying the wages of the workmen.

66. For employing poor artificers, and furnishing merchants and others with watches.

67. For improvement of tillage and the breed of cattle.

68. Another for the improvement of our breed of horses.

69. Another for a horse-insurance.

70. For carrying on the corn trade of Great Britain.

71. For insuring to all masters and mistresses the losses they may sustain by servants. Capital, three millions.

72. For erecting houses or hospitals, for taking in and maintaining illegitimate children. Capital, two millions.

73. For bleaching coarse sugars, without the use of fire or loss of substance.

74. For building turnpikes and wharfs in Great Britain.

75. For insuring from thefts and robberies.

76. For extracting silver from lead.

77. For making china and delft ware. Capital, one million.

78. For importing tobacco, and exporting it again to Sweden and the north of Europe. Capital, four millions.

79. For making iron with pit coal.

80. For furnishing the cities of London and Westminster with hay and straw. Capital, three millions.

81. For a sail and packing-cloth manufactory in Ireland.

82. For taking up ballast.

83. For buying and fitting out ships to suppress pirates.

84. For the importation of timber from Wales. Capital, two millions.

85. For rock-salt.

86. For the transmutation of quicksilver into a malleable fine metal.

Besides these bubbles, many others sprang up daily, in spite of the condemnation of the government and the ridicule of the still sane portion of the public. The print-shops teemed with caricatures, and the newspapers with epigrams and satires, upon the prevalent folly. An ingenious card-maker published a pack of South-Sea playing-cards, which are now extremely rare, each card containing, besides the usual figures, of a very small size, in one corner, a caricature of a bubble company, with appropriate verses underneath. One of the most famous bubbles was 'Puckle's Machine Company', for discharging round and square cannon-balls and bullets, and making a total revolution in the art of war. Its pretensions to public favour were thus summed up, on the eight of spades:

A rare invention to destroy the crowd
Of fools at home, instead of fools abroad.
Fear not, my friends, this terrible machine,
They're only wounded who have shares therein.

The nine of hearts was a caricature of the English Copper and Brass Company, with the following epigram:

The headlong fool that wants to be a swopper
Of gold and silver coin for English copper,

May, in Change Alley, prove himself an ass,
And give rich metal for adulterate brass.

The eight of diamonds celebrated the company for the colonisation of Acadia, with this doggerel:

He that is rich and wants to fool away
A good round sum in North America,
Let him subscribe himself a headlong sharer,
And asses' ears shall honour him or bearer.

And in a similar style every card of the pack exposed some knavish scheme, and ridiculed the persons who were its dupes. It was computed that the total amount of the sums proposed for carrying on these projects was upwards of three hundred millions sterling.

It is time, however, to return to the great South-Sea gulf, that swallowed the fortunes of so many thousands of the avaricious and the credulous. On the 29th of May, the stock had risen as high as five hundred, and about two-thirds of the government annuitants had exchanged the securities of the state for those of the South-Sea Company. During the whole of the month of May the stock continued to rise, and on the 28th it was quoted at five hundred and fifty. In four days after this it took a prodigious leap, rising suddenly from five hundred and fifty to eight hundred and ninety. It was now the general opinion that the stock could rise no higher, and many persons took that opportunity of selling out, with a view of realising their profits. Many noblemen and persons in the train of the king, and about to accompany him to Hanover, were also anxious to sell out. So many sellers, and so few buyers, appeared in the Alley on the 3rd of June, that the stock fell at once from eight hundred and ninety to six hundred and forty. The directors were alarmed, and gave their agents orders to buy. Their efforts succeeded. Towards evening confidence was restored, and the stock advanced to seven hundred and fifty. It continued at this price, with some slight fluctuation, until the company closed their books on the 22nd of June.

It would be needless and uninteresting to detail the various arts employed by the directors to keep up the price of stock. It will be sufficient to state that it finally rose to one thousand per cent. It was quoted at this price in the commencement of August. The bubble was then full-blown, and began to quiver and shake, preparatory to its bursting.

Many of the government annuitants expressed dissatisfaction against the directors. They accused them of partiality in making out the lists for shares in each subscription. Further uneasiness was occasioned by its being generally known that Sir John Blunt, the chairman, and some others, had sold out. During the whole of the month of August the stock fell, and on the 2nd of September it was quoted at seven hundred only.

The state of things now became alarming. To prevent, if possible, the utter extinction of public confidence in their proceedings, the directors summoned a general court of the whole corporation, to meet in Merchant Tailors' Hall on the 8th of September. By nine o'clock in the morning, the room was filled to suffocation; Cheapside was blocked up by a crowd unable to gain admittance, and the greatest excitement prevailed. The directors and their friends mustered in great numbers. Sir John Fellowes, the sub-governor, was called to the chair. He acquainted the assembly with the cause of their meeting; read to them the several resolutions of the court of directors, and gave them an account of their proceedings; of the taking in the redeemable and unredeemable funds, and of the subscriptions in money. Mr Secretary Craggs then made a short speech, wherein he commended the conduct of the directors, and urged that nothing could more effectually contribute to the bringing this scheme to perfection than union among themselves. He concluded with a motion for thanking the court of directors for their prudent and skilful management, and for desiring them to proceed in such manner as they should think most proper for the interest and advantage of the corporation. Mr Hungerford, who had rendered himself very conspicuous in the House of Commons for his zeal in behalf of the South-Sea Company, and who was shrewdly suspected to have been a considerable gainer by knowing the right time to sell out, was very magniloquent on this occasion. He said that he had seen the rise and fall, the decay and resurrection of many communities of this nature, but that, in his opinion, none had ever performed such wonderful things in so short a time as the South-Sea Company. They had done more than the crown, the pulpit, or the bench could do. They had reconciled all parties in one common interest; they had laid asleep, if not wholly extinguished, all the domestic jars and animosities of the nation. By the rise of their stock, monied men had vastly increased their fortunes;

country gentlemen had seen the value of their lands doubled and trebled in their hands. They had at the same time done good to the Church, not a few of the reverend clergy having got great sums by the project. In short, they had enriched the whole nation, and he hoped they had not forgotten themselves. There was some hissing at the latter part of this speech, which for the extravagance of its eulogy was not far removed from satire; but the directors and their friends, and all the winners in the room, applauded vehemently. The Duke of Portland spoke in a similar strain, and expressed his great wonder why anybody should be dissatisfied: of course, he was a winner by his speculations, and in a condition similar to that of the fat alderman in Joe Miller's *Jests*, who, whenever he had eaten a good dinner, folded his hands upon his paunch, and expressed his doubts whether there could be a hungry man in the world.

Several resolutions were passed at this meeting, but they had no effect upon the public. Upon the very same evening the stock fell to six hundred and forty, and on the morrow to five hundred and forty. Day after day it continued to fall, until it was as low as four hundred. In a letter, dated September 13th, from Mr Broderick MP to Lord Chancellor Middleton, and published in Coxe's *Walpole*, the former says: 'Various are the conjectures why the South-Sea directors have suffered the cloud to break so early. I made no doubt but they would do so when they found it to their advantage. They have stretched credit so far beyond what it would bear, that specie proves insufficient to support it. Their most considerable men have drawn out, securing themselves by the losses of the deluded, thoughtless numbers, whose understandings have been overruled by avarice and the hope of making mountains out of molehills. Thousands of families will be reduced to beggary. The consternation is inexpressible – the rage beyond description, and the case altogether so desperate that I do not see any plan or scheme so much as thought of for averting the blow, so that I cannot pretend to guess what is next to be done.' Ten days afterwards, the stock still falling, he writes: 'The company have yet come to no determination, for they are in such a wood that they know not which way to turn. By several gentlemen lately come to town, I perceive the very name of a South-Sea-man grows abominable in every country. A great many goldsmiths are already run off, and more will daily. I question whether one-third, nay, one-fourth, of them can stand it. From the very beginning, I founded my judgement of the whole affair upon the unquestionable maxim, that ten millions (which is more than our running cash) could not circulate two hundred millions, beyond which our paper credit extended. That, therefore, whenever that should become doubtful, be the cause what it would, our noble state machine must inevitably fall to the ground.'

On the 12th of September, at the earnest solicitation of Mr Secretary Craggs, several conferences were held between the directors of the South Sea and the directors of the Bank. A report which was circulated, that the latter had agreed to circulate six millions of the South-Sea Company's bonds, caused the stock to rise to six hundred and seventy; but in the afternoon, as soon as the report was known to be groundless, the stock fell again to five hundred and eighty; the next day to five hundred and seventy, and so gradually to four hundred.*

The ministry were seriously alarmed at the aspect of affairs. The directors could not appear in the streets without being insulted; dangerous riots were every moment apprehended. Despatches were sent off to the king at Hanover, praying his immediate return. Mr Walpole, who was staying at his country seat, was sent for, that he might employ his known influence with the directors of the Bank of England to induce them to accept the proposal made by the South-Sea Company for circulating a number of their bonds.

The Bank was very unwilling to mix itself up with the affairs of the company; it dreaded being involved in calamities which it could not relieve, and received all overtures with visible reluctance. But the universal voice of the nation called upon it to come to the rescue. Every person of note in commercial politics was called in to advise in the emergency. A rough draft of a contract drawn up by Mr Walpole was ultimately adopted as the basis of further negotiations, and the public alarm abated a little.

* Gay (the poet), in that disastrous year, had a present from young Craggs of some South-Sea stock, and once supposed himself to be master of twenty thousand pounds. His friends persuaded him to sell his share, but he dreamed of dignity and splendour, and could not bear to obstruct his own fortune. He was then importuned to sell as much as would purchase a hundred a year for life, 'which,' says Fenton, 'will make you sure of a clean shirt and a shoulder of mutton every day.' This counsel was rejected; the profit and principal were lost, and Gay sunk under the calamity so low that his life became in danger. – Johnson's *Lives of the Poets*.

On the following day, the 20th of September, a general court of the South-Sea Company was held at Merchant Tailors' Hall, in which resolutions were carried, empowering the directors to agree with the Bank of England, or any other persons, to circulate the company's bonds, or make any other agreement with the bank which they should think proper. One of the speakers, a Mr Pulteney, said it was most surprising to see the extraordinary panic which had seized upon the people. Men were running to and fro in alarm and terror, their imaginations filled with some great calamity, the form and dimensions of which nobody knew:

> Black it stood as night –
> Fierce as ten furies – terrible as hell.

At a general court of the Bank of England held two days afterwards, the governor informed them of the several meetings that had been held on the affairs of the South-Sea Company, adding that the directors had not yet thought fit to come to any decision upon the matter. A resolution was then proposed, and carried without a dissentient voice, empowering the directors to agree with those of the South Sea to circulate their bonds, to what sum, and upon what terms, and for what time, they might think proper.

Thus both parties were at liberty to act as they might judge best for the public interest. Books were opened at the Bank for a subscription of three millions for the support of public credit, on the usual terms of £15 per cent deposit, £3 per cent premium, and £5 per cent interest.

So great was the concourse of people in the early part of the morning, all eagerly bringing their money, that it was thought the subscription would be filled that day; but before noon, the tide turned. In spite of all that could be done to prevent it, the South-Sea Company's stock fell rapidly. Their bonds were in such discredit, that a run commenced upon the most eminent goldsmiths and bankers, some of whom having lent out great sums upon South-Sea stock were obliged to shut up their shops and abscond. The Sword-blade Company, who had hitherto been the chief cashiers of the South-Sea Company, stopped payment. This being looked upon as but the beginning of evil, occasioned a great run upon the Bank, who were now obliged to pay out money much faster than they had received it upon the subscription in the morning. The day succeeding was a holiday (the 29th of September), and the Bank had a little breathing time. They bore up against the storm; but their former rivals, the South-Sea Company, were wrecked upon it. Their stock fell to one hundred and fifty, and gradually, after various fluctuations, to one hundred and thirty-five.

The Bank, finding they were not able to restore public confidence, and stem the tide of ruin, without running the risk of being swept away with those they intended to save, declined to carry out the agreement into which they had partially entered. They were under no obligation whatever to continue; for the so-called Bank contract was nothing more than the rough draught of an agreement, in which blanks had been left for several important particulars, and which contained no penalty for their secession. 'And thus,' to use the words of the Parliamentary

History, 'were seen, in the space of eight months, the rise, progress, and fall of that mighty fabric, which, being wound up by mysterious springs to a wonderful height, had fixed the eyes and expectations of all Europe, but whose foundation, being fraud, illusion, credulity, and infatuation, fell to the ground as soon as the artful management of its directors was discovered.'

In the heyday of its blood, during the progress of this dangerous delusion, the manners of the nation became sensibly corrupted. The parliamentary inquiry, set on foot to discover the delinquents, disclosed scenes of infamy, disgraceful alike to the morals of the offenders and the intellects of the people among whom they had arisen. It is a deeply interesting study to investigate all the evils that were the result. Nations, like individuals, cannot become desperate gamblers with impunity. Punishment is sure to overtake them sooner or later. A celebrated writer* is quite wrong, when he says, 'that such an era as this is the most unfavourable for a historian; that no reader of sentiment and imagination can be entertained or interested by a detail of transactions such as these, which admit of no warmth, no colouring, no embellishment; a detail of which only serves to exhibit an inanimate picture of tasteless vice and mean degeneracy.' On the contrary – and Smollett might have discovered it, if he had been in the humour – the subject is capable of inspiring as much interest as even a novelist can desire. Is there no warmth in the despair of a plundered people? – no life and animation in the picture which might be

* Smollett.

drawn of the woes of hundreds of impoverished and ruined families? of the wealthy of yesterday become the beggars of today? of the powerful and influential changed into exiles and outcasts, and the voice of self-reproach and imprecation resounding from every corner of the land? Is it a dull or uninstructive picture to see a whole people shaking suddenly off the trammels of reason, and running wild after a golden vision, refusing obstinately to believe that it is not real, till, like a deluded hind running after an *ignis fatuus*, they are plunged into a quagmire? But in this false spirit has history too often been written. The intrigues of unworthy courtiers to gain the favour of still more unworthy kings; or the records of murderous battles and sieges have been dilated on, and told over and over again, with all the eloquence of style and all the charms of fancy; while the circumstances which have most deeply affected the morals and welfare of the people have been passed over with but slight notice as dry and dull, and capable of neither warmth nor colouring.

During the progress of this famous bubble, England presented a singular spectacle. The public mind was in a state of unwholesome fermentation. Men were no longer satisfied with the slow but sure profits of cautious industry. The hope of boundless wealth for the morrow made them heedless and extravagant for today. A luxury, till then unheard-of, was introduced, bringing in its train a corresponding laxity of morals. The overbearing insolence of ignorant men, who had arisen to sudden wealth by successful gambling, made men of true gentility of mind and manners blush that gold should have power to raise the unworthy in the scale of society. The haughtiness of some of these 'cyphering cits', as they were termed by Sir Richard Steele, was remembered against them in the day of their adversity. In the parliamentary inquiry, many of the directors suffered more for their insolence than for their peculation. One of them, who, in the full-blown pride of an ignorant rich man, had said that he would feed his horse upon gold, was reduced almost to bread and water for himself; every haughty look, every overbearing speech, was set down, and repaid them a hundredfold in poverty and humiliation.

The state of matters all over the country was so alarming, that George I shortened his intended stay in Hanover, and returned in all haste to England. He arrived on the 11th of November, and parliament was summoned to meet on the 8th of December. In the mean time, public meetings were held in every considerable town of the empire, at which petitions were adopted, praying the vengeance of the Legislature upon the South-Sea directors, who, by their fraudulent practices, had brought the nation to the brink of ruin. Nobody seemed to imagine that the nation itself was as culpable as the South-Sea Company. Nobody blamed the credulity and avarice of the people – the degrading lust of gain, which had swallowed up every nobler quality in the national character, or the infatuation which had made the multitude run their heads with such frantic eagerness into the net held out for them by scheming projectors. These things were never mentioned. The people were a simple, honest, hard-working people, ruined by a gang of robbers, who were to be hanged, drawn, and quartered without mercy.

This was the almost unanimous feeling of the country.

The two Houses of Parliament were not more reasonable. Before the guilt of the South-Sea directors was known, punishment was the only cry. The king, in his speech from the throne, expressed his hope that they would remember that all their prudence, temper, and resolution were necessary to find out and apply the proper remedy for their misfortunes. In the debate on the answer to the address, several speakers indulged in the most violent invectives against the directors of the South-Sea project. The Lord Molesworth was particularly vehement. 'It had been said by some, that there was no law to punish the directors of the South-Sea Company, who were justly looked upon as the authors of the present misfortunes of the state. In his opinion they ought upon this occasion to follow the example of the ancient Romans, who, having no law against parricide, because their legislators supposed no son could be so unnaturally wicked as to embrue his hands in his father's blood, made a law to punish this heinous crime as soon as it was committed. They adjudged the guilty wretch to be sown in a sack, and thrown alive into the Tiber. He looked upon the contrivers and executors of the villainous South-Sea scheme as the parricides of their country, and should be satisfied to see them tied in like manner in sacks, and thrown into the Thames.' Other members spoke with as much want of temper and discretion. Mr Walpole was more moderate. He recommended that their first care should be to restore public credit. 'If the city of London were on fire, all wise men would aid in extinguishing the flames, and preventing the spread of the conflagration before they enquired after the incendiaries. Public credit had received a dangerous wound, and lay bleeding, and they ought to apply a speedy remedy to it. It was time enough to punish the assassin afterwards.' On the 9th of December an address, in answer to his majesty's speech, was agreed upon, after an amendment, which was carried without a division, that words should be added expressive of the determination of the house not only to seek a remedy for the national distresses, but to punish the authors of them.

The inquiry proceeded rapidly. The directors were ordered to lay before the house a full account of all their proceedings. Resolutions were passed to the effect that the calamity was mainly owing to the vile arts of stock-jobbers, and that nothing could tend more to the re-establishment of public credit than a law to prevent this infamous practice. Mr Walpole then rose, and said, that 'as he had previously hinted, he had spent some time upon a scheme for restoring public credit, but that the execution of it depending upon a position which had been laid down as fundamental, he thought it proper, before he opened out his scheme, to be informed whether he might rely upon that foundation. It was, whether the subscription of public debts and encumbrances, money subscriptions, and other contracts, made with the South-Sea Company should remain in the present state?' This question occasioned an animated debate. It was finally agreed, by a majority of 259 against 117, that all these contracts should remain in their present state, unless altered for the relief of the proprietors by a general court of the South-Sea Company, or set aside by due course of law. On the following day Mr Walpole laid before a committee of the whole house his scheme for the restoration of public credit, which was, in substance, to engraft nine millions of South-Sea stock into the Bank of England, and the same sum into the East India Company, upon certain conditions. The plan was favourably received by the house. After some few objections, it was ordered that proposals should be received from the two great corporations. They were both unwilling to lend their aid, and the plan met with a warm but fruitless opposition at the general courts summoned for the purpose of deliberating upon it. They, however, ultimately agreed upon the terms on which they would consent to circulate the South-Sea bonds, and their report, being presented to the committee, a bill was brought in, under the superintendence of Mr Walpole, and safely carried through both Houses of Parliament.

A bill was at the same time brought in, for restraining the South-Sea directors, governor, sub-governor, treasurer, cashier, and clerks from leaving the kingdom for a twelvemonth, and for discovering their estates and effects, and preventing them from transporting or alienating the same. All the most influential members of the house supported the bill. Mr Shippen, seeing Mr Secretary Craggs in his place, and believing the injurious rumours that were afloat of that minister's conduct in the South-Sea business, determined to touch him to the quick. He said, he was glad to see a British House of Commons resuming its pristine vigour and spirit, and acting with so much unanimity for the public good. It was necessary to secure the persons and estates of the South-Sea directors and their officers; 'but,' he added, looking fixedly at Mr Craggs as he spoke, 'there were other men in high station, whom, in time, he would not be afraid to name, who were no less guilty than the directors.' Mr Craggs arose in great wrath, and said, that if the innuendo were directed against him, he was ready to give satisfaction to any man who questioned him, either in the House or out of it. Loud cries of order immediately arose on every side. In the midst of the uproar Lord Molesworth got up, and expressed his wonder at the boldness of Mr Craggs in challenging the whole House of Commons. He, Lord Molesworth, though somewhat old, past sixty, would answer Mr Craggs whatever he had to say in the House, and he trusted there were plenty of young men beside him, who would not be afraid to look Mr Craggs in the face, out of the House. The cries of order again resounded from every side; the members arose simultaneously; everybody seemed to be vociferating at once. The speaker in vain called order. The confusion lasted several minutes, during which Lord Molesworth and Mr Craggs were almost the only members who kept their seats. At last, the call for Mr Craggs became so violent that he thought proper to submit to the universal feeling of the House, and explain his unparliamentary expression. He said, that by giving satisfaction to the impugners of his conduct in that House, he did not mean that he would fight, but that he would explain his conduct. Here the matter ended, and the House proceeded to debate in what manner they should conduct their inquiry into the affairs of the South-Sea Company, whether in a grand or a select committee. Ultimately, a secret committee of thirteen was appointed, with power to send for persons, papers, and records.

The Lords were as zealous and as hasty as the Commons. The Bishop of Rochester said the scheme had been like a pestilence. The Duke of Wharton said the House ought to show no respect of persons; that, for his part, he would give up the dearest friend he had, if he had been engaged in the project. The nation had been plundered in a most shameful and flagrant manner, and he would go as far as anybody in the punishment of the offenders. Lord Stanhope said, that every farthing possessed by the criminals, whether directors or not directors, ought to be confiscated, to make good the public losses.

During all this time the public excitement was extreme. We learn, from Coxe's *Walpole*, that the very name of a South-Sea director was thought to be synonymous with every species of fraud and villainy. Petitions from counties, cities, and boroughs, in all parts of the kingdom, were presented, crying for the justice due to an injured nation and the punishment of the villainous peculators. Those moderate men, who would not go to extreme lengths, even in the punishment of the guilty, were accused of being accomplices, were exposed to repeated insults and virulent invectives, and devoted, both in anonymous letters and public writings, to the speedy vengeance of an injured people. The accusations against Mr Aislabie, Chancellor of the Exchequer, and Mr Craggs, another member of the ministry, were so loud, that the House of Lords resolved to proceed at once into the investigation concerning them. It was ordered, on the 21st of January, that all brokers concerned in the South-Sea scheme should lay before the house an account of the stock or subscriptions bought or sold by them for any of the officers of the Treasury or Exchequer, or in trust for any of them, since Michaelmas 1719. When this account was delivered, it appeared that large quantities of stock had been transferred to the use of Mr Aislabie. Five of the South-Sea directors, including Mr Edward Gibbon, the grandfather of the celebrated historian, were ordered into the custody of the black rod. Upon a motion made by Earl Stanhope, it was unanimously resolved, that the taking in or giving credit for stock without a valuable consideration actually paid or sufficiently secured; or the purchasing stock by any director or agent of the South-Sea Company, for the use or benefit of any member of the administration, or any member of either House of Parliament, during such time as the South-Sea bill was yet pending in parliament, was a notorious and dangerous corruption. Another resolution was passed a few days afterwards, to the effect that several of the directors and officers of the company having, in a clandestine manner, sold their own stock to the company, had been guilty of a notorious fraud and breach of trust, and had thereby mainly caused the unhappy turn of affairs that had so much affected public credit. Mr Aislabie resigned his office as Chancellor of the Exchequer, and absented himself from parliament until the formal inquiry into his individual guilt was brought under the consideration of the legislature.

In the mean time, Knight, the treasurer of the company, and who was entrusted with all the dangerous secrets of the dishonest directors, packed up his books and documents, and made his escape from the country. He embarked in disguise, in a small boat on the river, and proceeding to a vessel hired for the purpose, was safely conveyed to Calais. The Committee of Secrecy informed the House of the circumstance, when it was resolved unanimously that two addresses should be presented to the king; the first praying that he would issue a proclamation offering a reward for the apprehension of Knight; and the second, that he would give immediate orders to stop the ports, and to take effectual care of the coasts, to prevent the said Knight, or any other officers of the South-Sea Company, from escaping out of the kingdom. The ink was hardly dry upon these addresses before they were carried to the king by Mr Methuen, deputed by the House for that purpose. The same evening a royal proclamation was issued, offering a reward of two thousand pounds for the apprehension of Knight. The Commons ordered the doors of the House to be locked, and the keys to be placed upon the table. General Ross, one of the members of the Committee of Secrecy, acquainted them that they had already discovered a train of the deepest villainy and fraud that hell had ever contrived to ruin a nation, which in due time they would lay before the House. In the mean time, in order to a further discovery, the Committee thought it highly necessary to secure the persons of some of the directors and principal South-Sea officers, and to seize their papers. A motion to this effect having been made, was carried unanimously. Sir Robert Chaplin, Sir Theodore Janssen, Mr Sawbridge, and Mr F. Eyles, members of the House, and directors of the South-Sea Company, were summoned to appear in their places, and answer for their corrupt practices. Sir Theodore Janssen and Mr Sawbridge answered to their names, and endeavoured to exculpate themselves. The House heard them patiently, and then ordered them to withdraw.

A motion was then made, and carried *nemine contra-dicente*, that they had been guilty of a notorious breach of trust – had occasioned much loss to great numbers of his majesty's subjects, and had highly prejudiced the public credit. It was then ordered that, for their offence, they should be expelled the House, and taken into the custody of the sergeant-at-arms. Sir Robert Chaplin and Mr Eyles, attending in their places four days afterwards, were also expelled the House. It was resolved at the same time to address the king to give directions to his ministers at foreign courts to make application for Knight, that he might be delivered up to the English authorities, in case he took refuge in any of their dominions. The king at once agreed, and messengers were despatched to all parts of the Continent the same night.

Among the directors taken into custody, was Sir John Blunt, the man whom popular opinion has generally accused of having been the original author and father of the scheme. This man, we are informed by Pope, in his epistle to Allen, Lord Bathurst, was a dissenter, of a most religious deportment, and professed to be a great believer. He constantly declaimed against the luxury and corruption of the age, the partiality of parliaments, and the misery of party spirit. He was particularly eloquent against avarice in great and noble persons. He was originally a scrivener, and afterwards became, not only a director, but the most active manager of the South-Sea Company. Whether it was during his career in this capacity that he first began to declaim against the avarice of the great, we are not informed. He certainly must have seen enough of it to justify his severest anathema; but if the preacher had

himself been free from the vice he condemned, his dec-
lamations would have had a better effect. He was brought
up in custody to the bar of the House of Lords, and
underwent a long examination. He refused to answer
several important questions. He said he had been examined already by a committee of the House of Commons,
and as he did not remember his answers, and might con-
tradict himself, he refused to answer before another tri-
bunal. This declaration, in itself an indirect proof of
guilt, occasioned some commotion in the House. He was
again asked peremptorily whether he had ever sold any
portion of the stock to any member of the administration, or any member of either House of Parliament, to
facilitate the passing of the bill. He again declined to
answer. He was anxious, he said, to treat the House with all
possible respect, but he thought it hard to be compelled
to accuse himself. After several ineffectual attempts to
refresh his memory, he was directed to withdraw. A
violent discussion ensued between the friends and opponents of the ministry. It was asserted that the administration were no strangers to the convenient taciturnity of
Sir John Blunt. The Duke of Wharton made a reflection
upon the Earl Stanhope, which the latter warmly resented.
He spoke under great excitement, and with such vehe-
mence as to cause a sudden determination of blood to
the head. He felt himself so ill that he was obliged to
leave the House and retire to his chamber. He was cup-
ped immediately, and also let blood on the following
morning, but with slight relief. The fatal result was not
anticipated. Towards evening he became drowsy, and
turning himself on his face, expired. The sudden death

of this statesman caused great grief to the nation. George I was exceedingly affected, and shut himself up for some hours in his closet, inconsolable for his loss.

Knight, the treasurer of the company, was apprehended at Tirlemont, near Liège, by one of the secretaries of Mr Leathes, the British resident at Brussels, and lodged in the citadel of Antwerp. Repeated applications were made to the court of Austria to deliver him up, but in vain. Knight threw himself upon the protection of the states of Brabant, and demanded to be tried in that country. It was a privilege granted to the states of Brabant by one of the articles of the *Foyeuse Entrée*, that every criminal apprehended in that country should be tried in that country. The states insisted on their privilege, and refused to deliver Knight to the British authorities. The latter did not cease their solicitations; but in the mean time, Knight escaped from the citadel.

On the 16th of February the Committee of Secrecy made their first report to the House. They stated that their inquiry had been attended with numerous difficulties and embarrassments; everyone they had examined had endeavoured, as far as in him lay, to defeat the ends of justice. In some of the books produced before them, false and fictitious entries had been made; in others, there were entries of money, with blanks for the name of the stockholders. There were frequent erasures and alterations, and in some of the books leaves were torn out. They also found that some books of great importance had been destroyed altogether, and that some had been taken away or secreted. At the very entrance into their inquiry, they had observed that the matters referred to them were of great variety and extent. Many persons had been entrusted with various parts in the execution of the law, and under colour thereof had acted in an unwarrantable manner, in disposing of the properties of many thousands of persons, amounting to many millions of money. They discovered that, before the South-Sea Act was passed, there was an entry in the company's books of the sum of £1,259,325, upon account of stock stated to have been sold to the amount of £574,500. This stock was all fictitious, and had been disposed of with a view to promote the passing of the bill. It was noted as sold at various days, and at various prices, from 150 to 325 per cent. Being surprised to see so large an account disposed of, at a time when the company were not empowered to increase their capital, the Committee determined to investigate most carefully the whole transaction. The governor, sub-governor, and several directors were brought before them, and examined rigidly. They found that, at the time these entries were made, the company was not in possession of such a quantity of stock, having in their own right only a small quantity, not exceeding thirty thousand pounds at the utmost. Pursuing the inquiry, they found that this amount of stock was to be esteemed as taken in or holden by the company for the benefit of the pretended purchasers, although no mutual agreement was made for its delivery or acceptance at any certain time. No money was paid down, nor any deposit or security whatever given to the company by the supposed purchasers; so that if the stock had fallen, as might have been expected, had the act not passed, they would have sustained no loss. If, on the contrary, the price of stock advanced (as it actually did by the success of the scheme), the difference by the advanced price was to be made good to them. Accordingly, after the passing of the act, the account of stock was made up and adjusted with Mr Knight, and the pretended purchasers were paid the difference out of the company's cash. This fictitious stock, which had been chiefly at the disposal of Sir John Blunt, Mr Gibbon, and Mr Knight, was distributed among several members of the government and their connections, by way of bribe, to facilitate the passing of the bill. To the Earl of Sunderland was assigned £50,000 of this stock; to the Duchess of Kendal £10,000; to the Countess of Platen £10,000; to her two nieces £10,000; to Mr Secretary Craggs £30,000; to Mr Charles Stanhope (one of the secretaries of the Treasury) £10,000; to the Sword-blade company £50,000. It also appeared that Mr Stanhope had received the enormous sum of £250,000 as the difference in the price of some stock, through the hands of Turner, Caswall, and Co., but that his name had been partly erased from their books, and altered to Stangape. Aislabie, the Chancellor of the Exchequer, had made profits still more abominable. He had an account with the same firm, who were also South-Sea directors, to the amount of £794,451. He had, besides, advised the company to make their second subscription one million and a half, instead of a million, by their own authority, and without any warrant. The third subscription had been conducted in a manner as disgraceful. Mr Aislabie's name was down for £70,000; Mr Craggs, senior, for £659,000; the Earl of Sunderland's for £160,000; and Mr Stanhope for £47,000. This report was succeeded by six others, less important. At the end of the last, the committee declared that the absence of Knight, who had been principally entrusted, prevented them from carrying on their enquiries.

The first report was ordered to be printed, and taken into consideration on the next day but one succeeding. After a very angry and animated debate, a series of resolutions were agreed to, condemnatory of the conduct of the directors, of the members of the parliament and of the administration concerned with them; and declaring that they ought, each and all, to make satisfaction out of their own estates for the injury they had done the public. Their practices were declared to be corrupt, infamous, and dangerous; and a bill was ordered to be brought in for the relief of the unhappy sufferers.

Mr Charles Stanhope was the first person brought to account for his share in these transactions. He urged in his defence that, for some years past, he had lodged all the money he was possessed of in Mr Knight's hands, and whatever stock Mr Knight had taken in for him, he had paid a valuable consideration for it. As to the stock that had been bought for him by Turner, Caswall, and Co., he knew nothing about it. Whatever had been done in that matter was done without his authority, and he could not be responsible for it. Turner and Co. took the latter charge upon themselves; but it was notorious to every unbiassed and unprejudiced person that Mr Stanhope was a gainer of the £250,000 which lay in the hands of that firm to his credit. He was, however, acquitted by a majority of three only. The greatest exertions were made to screen him. Lord Stanhope, the son of the Earl of Chesterfield, went round to the wavering members, using all the eloquence he was possessed of to induce them either to vote for the acquittal or to absent themselves from the House. Many weak-headed country gentlemen were led astray by his persuasions, and the result was as already stated. The acquittal caused the greatest discontent throughout the country. Mobs of a menacing character assembled in different parts of London; fears of riots were generally entertained, especially as the examination of a still greater delinquent was expected by many to have a similar termination. Mr Aislabie, whose high office and deep responsibilities should have kept him honest, even had native principle been insufficient, was very justly regarded as perhaps the greatest criminal of all. His case was entered into on the day succeeding the acquittal of Mr Stanhope. Great excitement prevailed, and the lobbies and avenues of the House were beset by crowds, impatient to know the result. The debate lasted the whole day. Mr Aislabie found few friends: his guilt was so apparent and so heinous that nobody had courage to stand up in his favour. It was finally resolved, without a dissentient voice, that Mr Aislabie had encouraged and promoted the destructive execution of the South-Sea scheme with a view to his own exorbitant profit, and had combined with the directors in their pernicious practices, to the ruin of the public trade and credit of the kingdom: that he should for his offences be ignominiously expelled from the House of Commons, and committed a close prisoner to the Tower of London; that he should be restrained from going out of the kingdom for a whole year, or till the end of the next session of Parliament; and that he should make out a correct account of all his estate, in order that it might be applied to the relief of those who had suffered by his malpractices.

This verdict caused the greatest joy. Though it was delivered at half-past twelve at night, it soon spread over the city. Several persons illuminated their houses in token of their joy. On the following day, when Mr Aislabie was conveyed to the Tower, the mob assembled on Tower-hill with the intention of hooting and pelting him. Not succeeding in this, they kindled a large bonfire, and danced around it in the exuberance of their delight. Several bonfires were made in other places; London presented the appearance of a holiday, and people congratulated one another as if they had just escaped from some great calamity. The rage upon the acquittal of Mr Stanhope had grown to such a height that none could tell where it would have ended, had Mr Aislabie met with the like indulgence.

To increase the public satisfaction, Sir George Caswall, of the firm of Turner, Caswall, and Co., was expelled from the House on the following day, committed to the Tower, and ordered to refund the sum of £250,000.

That part of the report of the Committee of Secrecy which related to the Earl of Sunderland was next taken into consideration. Every effort was made to clear his lordship from the imputation. As the case against him rested chiefly on the evidence extorted from Sir John Blunt, great pains were taken to make it appear that Sir John's word was not to be believed, especially in a matter affecting the honour of a peer and privy councillor. All the friends of the ministry rallied around the earl, it being generally reported that a verdict of guilty against him would bring a Tory ministry into power. He was eventually acquitted by a majority of 233 against 172; but the country was convinced of his guilt. The greatest indignation was everywhere expressed, and menacing mobs again assembled in London. Happily no disturbances took place.

This was the day on which Mr Craggs the elder expired. The morrow had been appointed for the consideration of his case. It was very generally believed that he had poisoned himself. It appeared, however, that grief for the loss of his son, one of the secretaries of the Treasury, who had died five weeks previously of the smallpox, preyed much on his mind. For this son, dearly beloved, he had been amassing vast heaps of riches: he had been getting money, but not honestly; and he for whose sake he had bartered his honour and sullied his fame, was now no more. The dread of further exposure increased his trouble of mind, and ultimately brought on an apoplectic fit, in which he expired. He left a fortune of a million and a half, which was afterwards confiscated for the benefit of the sufferers by the unhappy delusion he had been so mainly instrumental in raising.

One by one the case of every director of the company was taken into consideration. A sum amounting to two millions and fourteen thousand pounds was confiscated from their estates towards repairing the mischief they had done, each man being allowed a certain residue, in proportion to his conduct and circumstances, with which he might begin the world anew. Sir John Blunt was only allowed £5,000 out of his fortune of upwards of £183,000; Sir John Fellows was allowed £10,000 out of £243,000; Sir

Theodore Janssen, £50,000 out of £243,000; Mr Edward Gibbon, £10,000 out of £106,000; Sir John Lambert, £5,000 out of £72,000. Others, less deeply involved, were treated with greater liberality. Gibbon, the historian, whose grandfather was the Mr Edward Gibbon so severely mulcted, has given, in the *Memoirs of his Life and Writings*, an interesting account of the proceedings in parliament at this time. He owns that he is not an unprejudiced witness; but, as all the writers from which it is possible to extract any notice of the proceedings of these disastrous years were prejudiced on the other side, the statements of the great historian become of additional value. If only on the principle of *audi alteram partem*, his opinion is entitled to consideration. 'In the year 1716,' he says, 'my grandfather was elected one of the directors of the South-Sea company, and his books exhibited the proof that before his acceptance of that fatal office, he had acquired an independent fortune of £60,000. But his fortune was overwhelmed in the shipwreck of the year 1720, and the labours of thirty years were blasted in a single day. Of the use or abuse of the South-Sea scheme, of the guilt or innocence of my grandfather and his brother directors, I am neither a competent nor a disinterested judge. Yet the equity of modern times must condemn the violent and arbitrary proceedings, which would have disgraced the cause of justice, and rendered injustice still more odious. No sooner had the nation awakened from its golden dream, than a popular, and even a parliamentary clamour demanded its victims; but it was acknowledged on all sides, that the directors, however guilty, could not be touched by any known laws of the land.

The intemperate notions of Lord Molesworth were not literally acted on; but a bill of pains and penalties was introduced – a retroactive statute, to punish the offences which did not exist at the time they were committed. The legislature restrained the persons of the directors, imposed an exorbitant security for their appearance, and marked their character with a previous note of ignominy. They were compelled to deliver, upon oath, the strict value of their estates, and were disabled from making any transfer or alienation of any part of their property. Against a bill of pains and penalties, it is the common right of every subject to be heard by his counsel at the bar. They prayed to be heard. Their prayer was refused, and their oppressors, who required no evidence, would listen to no defence. It had been at first proposed, that one-eighth of their respective estates should be allowed for the future support of the directors; but it was especially urged that, in the various shades of opulence and guilt, such a proportion would be too light for many, and for some might possibly be too heavy. The character and conduct of each man were separately weighed; but, instead of the calm solemnity of a judicial inquiry, the fortune and honour of thirty-three Englishmen were made the topics of hasty conversation, the sport of a lawless majority; and the basest member of the committee, by a malicious word, or a silent vote, might indulge his general spleen or personal animosity. Injury was aggravated by insult, and insult was embittered by pleasantry. Allowances of £20 or 1s. were facetiously moved. A vague report that a director had formerly been concerned in another project, by which some unknown persons had lost their money, was admitted as a proof of his actual guilt. One man was ruined because he had dropped a foolish speech, that his horses should feed upon gold; another, because he was grown so proud, that one day, at the Treasury, he had refused a civil answer to persons much above him. All were condemned, absent and unheard, in arbitrary fines and forfeitures, which swept away the greatest part of their substance. Such bold oppression can scarcely be shielded by the omnipotence of parliament. My grandfather could not expect to be treated with more lenity than his companions. His Tory principles and connections rendered him obnoxious to the ruling powers. His name was reported in a suspicious secret. His well-known abilities could not plead the excuse of ignorance or error. In the first proceedings against the South-Sea directors, Mr Gibbon was one of the first taken into custody, and in the final sentence the measure of his fine proclaimed him eminently guilty. The total estimate, which he delivered on oath to the House of Commons, amounted to £106,543 5s. 6d., exclusive of antecedent settlements. Two different allowances of £15,000 and of £10,000 were moved for Mr Gibbon; but, on the question being put, it was carried without a division for the smaller sum. On these ruins, with the skill and credit of which parliament had not been able to despoil him, my grandfather, at a mature age, erected the edifice of a new fortune. The labours of sixteen years were amply rewarded; and I have reason to believe that the second structure was not much inferior to the first.'

The next consideration of the legislature, after the punishment of the directors, was to restore public credit.

The scheme of Walpole had been found insufficient, and had fallen into disrepute. A computation was made of the whole capital stock of the South-Sea Company at the end of the year 1720. It was found to amount to thirty-seven millions eight hundred thousand pounds, of which the stock allotted to all the proprietors only amounted to twenty-four millions five hundred thousand pounds. The remainder of thirteen millions three hundred thousand pounds belonged to the company in their corporate capacity, and was the profit they had made by the national delusion. Upwards of eight millions of this were taken from the company, and divided among the proprietors and subscribers generally, making a dividend of about £33 6s. 8d. per cent. This was a great relief. It was further ordered, that such persons as had borrowed money from the South-Sea Company upon stock actually transferred and pledged at the time of borrowing to or for the use of the company, should be free from all demands, upon payment of ten per cent of the sums so borrowed. They had lent about eleven millions in this manner, at a time when prices were unnaturally raised; and they now received back one million one hundred thousand, when prices had sunk to their ordinary level.

But it was a long time before public credit was thoroughly restored. Enterprise, like Icarus, had soared too high, and melted the wax of her wings; like Icarus, she had fallen into a sea, and learned, while floundering in its waves, that her proper element was the solid ground. She has never since attempted so high a flight.

In times of great commercial prosperity there has been a tendency to over-speculation on several occasions since then. The success of one project generally produces others of a similar kind. Popular imitativeness will always, in a trading nation, seize hold of such successes, and drag a community too anxious for profits into an abyss from which extrication is difficult. Bubble companies, of a kind similar to those engendered by the South-Sea project, lived their little day in the famous year of the panic, 1825. On that occasion, as in 1720, knavery gathered a rich harvest from cupidity, but both suffered when the day of reckoning came. The schemes of the year 1836 threatened, at one time, results as disastrous; but they were happily averted before it was too late.*

* The South-Sea project remained until 1845 the greatest example in British history of the infatuation of the people for commercial gambling. The first edition of these volumes was published some time before the outbreak of the Great Railway Mania of that and the following year.

3
The Tulipomania

Quis furor ō cives!
Lucan

The tulip, so named, it is said, from a Turkish word, sig-
nifying a turban – was introduced into western Europe
about the middle of the sixteenth century. Conrad Gesner,
who claims the merit of having brought it into repute –
little dreaming of the extraordinary commotion it was to
make in the world – says that he first saw it in the year
1559, in a garden at Augsburg, belonging to the learned
Counsellor Herwart, a man very famous in his day for his
collection of rare exotics. The bulbs were sent to this
gentleman by a friend at Constantinople, where the flower
had long been a favourite. In the course of ten or eleven
years after this period, tulips were much sought after by
the wealthy, especially in Holland and Germany. Rich
people at Amsterdam sent for the bulbs direct to Constantinople, and paid the most extravagant prices for
them. The first roots planted in England were brought
from Vienna in 1600. Until the year 1634 the tulip annually
increased in reputation, until it was deemed a proof of
bad taste in any man of fortune to be without a collection of them. Many learned men, including Pompeius de
Angelis and the celebrated Lipsius of Leyden, the author

of the treatise 'De Constantia', were passionately fond of tulips. The rage for possessing them soon caught the middle classes of society, and merchants and shopkeepers, even of moderate means, began to vie with each other in the rarity of these flowers and the preposterous prices they paid for them. A trader at Harlaem was known to pay one-half of his fortune for a single root, not with the design of selling it again at a profit, but to keep in his own conservatory for the admiration of his acquaintance.

One would suppose that there must have been some great virtue in this flower to have made it so valuable in the eyes of so prudent a people as the Dutch; but it has neither the beauty nor the perfume of the rose – hardly the beauty of the 'sweet, sweet-pea'; neither is it as enduring as either. Cowley, it is true, is loud in its praise. He says:

> The tulip next appeared, all over gay,
> But wanton, full of pride, and full of play;
> The world can't show a dye but here has place;
> Nay, by new mixtures, she can change her face;
> Purple and gold are both beneath her care,
> The richest needlework she loves to wear;
> Her only study is to please the eye,
> And to outshine the rest in finery.

This, though not very poetical, is the description of a poet. Beckmann, in his *History of Inventions*, paints it with more fidelity, and in prose more pleasing than Cowley's poetry. He says,

There are few plants which acquire, through accident, weakness, or disease, so many variegations as the tulip. When uncultivated, and in its natural state, it is almost of one colour, has large leaves, and an extraordinarily long stem. When it has been weakened by cultivation, it becomes more agreeable in the eyes of the florist. The petals are then paler, smaller, and more diversified in hue; and the leaves acquire a softer green colour. Thus this masterpiece of culture, the more beautiful it turns, grows so much the weaker, so that, with the greatest skill and most careful attention, it can scarcely be transplanted, or even kept alive.

Many persons grow insensibly attached to that which gives them a great deal of trouble, as a mother often loves her sick and ever-ailing child better than her more healthy offspring. Upon the same principle we must account for the unmerited encomia lavished upon these fragile blossoms. In 1634, the rage among the Dutch to possess them was so great that the ordinary industry of the country was neglected, and the population, even to its lowest dregs, embarked in the tulip trade. As the mania increased, prices augmented, until, in the year 1635, many persons were known to invest a fortune of 100,000 florins in the purchase of forty roots. It then became necessary to sell them by their weight in perits, a small weight less than a grain. A tulip of the species called Admiral Liefken, weighing 400 perits, was worth 4,400 florins; an Admiral Van der Eyck, weighing 446 perits, was worth 1,260 florins; a Childer of 106 perits was worth 1,615 florins; a Viceroy of 400 perits, 3,000 florins, and, most precious of all, a Semper Augustus, weighing 200 perits, was thought to be very cheap at 5,500 florins. The latter was much sought after, and even an inferior bulb might command a price of 2,000 florins. It is related that, at one time, early in 1636, there were only two roots of this description to be had in all Holland, and those not of the best. One was in the possession of a dealer in Amsterdam, and the other in Harlaem. So anxious were the speculators to obtain them that one person offered the fee-simple of twelve acres of building ground for the Harlaem tulip. That of Amsterdam was bought for 4,600 florins, a new carriage, two grey horses, and a complete suit of harness. Munting, an industrious author of that day, who wrote a folio volume of one thousand pages upon the tulipomania, has preserved the following list of the various articles, and their value, which were delivered for one single root of the rare species called the Viceroy:

	florins
Two lasts of wheat	448
Four lasts of rye	558
Four fat oxen	480
Eight fat swine	240
Twelve fat sheep	120
Two hogsheads of wine	70
Four tuns of beer	32
Two tons of butter	192
One thousand lbs. of cheese	120
A complete bed	100
A suit of clothes	80
A silver drinking cup	60
	2,500

People who had been absent from Holland, and whose chance it was to return when this folly was at its maximum, were sometimes led into awkward dilemmas by their ignorance. There is an amusing instance of the kind related in Blainville's Travels. A wealthy merchant, who prided himself not a little on his rare tulips, received upon one occasion a very valuable consignment of merchandise from the Levant. Intelligence of its arrival was brought him by a sailor, who presented himself for that purpose at the counting-house, among bales of goods of every description. The merchant, to reward him for his news, munificently made him a present of a fine red herring for his breakfast. The sailor had, it appears, a great partiality for onions, and seeing a bulb very like an onion lying upon the counter of this liberal trader, and thinking it, no doubt, very much out of its place among silks and velvets, he slily seized an opportunity and slipped it into his pocket, as a relish for his herring. He got clear off with his prize, and proceeded to the quay to eat his breakfast. Hardly was his back turned when the merchant missed his valuable Semper Augustus, worth three thousand florins, or about £280 sterling. The whole establishment was instantly in an uproar; search was everywhere made for the precious root, but it was not to be found. Great was the merchant's distress of mind. The search was renewed, but again without success. At last someone thought of the sailor.

The unhappy merchant sprang into the street at the bare suggestion. His alarmed household followed him. The sailor, simple soul! had not thought of concealment. He was found quietly sitting on a coil of ropes, masticating the last morsel of his 'onion'. Little did he dream that he had been eating a breakfast whose cost might have regaled a whole ship's crew for a twelvemonth; or, as the plundered merchant himself expressed it, 'might have sumptuously feasted the Prince of Orange and the whole court of the Stadtholder'. Anthony caused pearls to be dissolved in wine to drink the health of Cleopatra; Sir Richard Whittington was as foolishly magnificent in an entertainment to King Henry V; and Sir Thomas Gresham drank a diamond, dissolved in wine, to the health of Queen Elizabeth, when she opened the Royal Exchange; but the breakfast of this roguish Dutchman was as splendid as either. He had an advantage, too, over his wasteful predecessors: *their* gems did not improve the taste or the wholesomeness of *their* wine, while *his* tulip was quite delicious with his red herring. The most unfortunate part of the business for him was that he remained in prison for some months on a charge of felony preferred against him by the merchant.

Another story is told of an English traveller, which is scarcely less ludicrous. This gentleman, an amateur botanist, happened to see a tulip-root lying in the conservatory of a wealthy Dutchman. Being ignorant of its quality, he took out his penknife, and peeled off its coats, with the view of making experiments upon it. When it was by this means reduced to half its original size, he cut it into two equal sections, making all the time many learned remarks on the singular appearances of the unknown bulb. Suddenly the owner pounced upon him, and, with fury in his eyes, asked him if he knew what he had been doing? 'Peeling a most extraordinary onion,' replied the philosopher.

'Hundert tausend duyvel!' said the Dutchman; 'it's an Admiral Van der Eyck.' 'Thank you,' replied the traveller, taking out his notebook to make a memorandum of the same; 'are these admirals common in your country?' 'Death and the devil,' said the Dutchman, seizing the astonished man of science by the collar; 'come before the syndic, and you shall see.' In spite of his remonstrances, the traveller was led through the streets, followed by a mob of persons. When brought into the presence of the magistrate, he learned, to his consternation, that the root upon which he had been experimentalising was worth four thousand florins; and, notwithstanding all he could urge in extenuation, he was lodged in prison until he found securities for the payment of this sum.

The demand for tulips of a rare species increased so much in the year 1636, that regular marts for their sale were established on the Stock Exchange of Amsterdam, in Rotterdam, Harlaem, Leyden, Alkmar, Hoorn, and other towns. Symptoms of gambling now became, for the first time, apparent. The stock-jobbers, ever on the alert for a new speculation, dealt largely in tulips, making use of all the means they so well knew how to employ, to cause fluctuations in prices. At first, as in all these gambling mania, confidence was at its height, and everybody gained. The tulip-jobbers speculated in the rise and fall of the tulip stocks, and made large profits by buying when prices fell, and selling out when they rose. Many individuals grew suddenly rich. A golden bait hung temptingly out before the people, and, one after the other, they rushed to the tulip marts, like flies around a honey-pot. Everyone imagined that the passion for tulips would last for ever, and that the wealthy from every part of the world would send to Holland, and pay whatever prices were asked for them. The riches of Europe would be concentrated on the shores of the Zuyder Zee, and poverty banished from the favoured clime of Holland. Nobles, citizens, farmers, mechanics, seamen, footmen, maidservants, even chimney-sweeps and old clotheswomen, dabbled in tulips. People of all grades converted their property into cash, and invested it in flowers. Houses and lands were offered for sale at ruinously low prices, or assigned in payment of bargains made at the tulip-mart. Foreigners became smitten with the same frenzy, and money poured into Holland from all directions. The prices of the necessaries of life rose again by degrees: houses and lands, horses and carriages, and luxuries of every sort, rose in value with them, and for some months Holland seemed the very antechamber of Plutus. The operations of the trade became so extensive and so intricate, that it was found necessary to draw up a code of laws for the guidance of the dealers. Notaries and clerks were also appointed, who devoted themselves exclusively to the interests of the trade. The designation of public notary was hardly known in some towns, that of tulip-notary usurping its place. In the smaller towns, where there was no exchange, the principal tavern was usually selected as the 'show-place', where high and low traded in tulips, and confirmed their bargains over sumptuous entertainments. These dinners were sometimes attended by two or three hundred persons, and large vases of tulips, in full bloom, were placed at regular intervals upon the tables and sideboards, for their gratification during the repast.

At last, however, the more prudent began to see that this folly could not last for ever. Rich people no longer bought the flowers to keep them in their gardens, but to sell them again at cent per cent profit. It was seen that somebody must lose fearfully in the end. As this conviction spread, prices fell, and never rose again. Confidence was destroyed, and a universal panic seized upon the dealers. A had agreed to purchase ten Sempers Augustines from B, at four thousand florins each, at six weeks after the signing of the contract. B was ready with the flowers at the appointed time; but the price had fallen to three or four hundred florins, and A refused either to pay the difference or receive the tulips. Defaulters were announced day after day in all the towns of Holland. Hundreds who, a few months previously, had begun to doubt that there was such a thing as poverty in the land, suddenly found themselves the possessors of a few bulbs, which nobody would buy, even though they offered them at one quarter of the sums they had paid for them. The cry of distress resounded everywhere, and each man accused his neighbour. The few who had contrived to enrich themselves hid their wealth from the knowledge of their fellow-citizens, and invested it in the English or other funds. Many who, for a brief season, had emerged from the humbler walks of life, were cast back into their original obscurity. Substantial merchants were reduced almost to beggary, and many a representative of a noble line saw the fortunes of his house ruined beyond redemption.

When the first alarm subsided, the tulip-holders in the several towns held public meetings to devise what measures were best to be taken to restore public credit. It was generally agreed, that deputies should be sent from all parts to Amsterdam, to consult with the government upon some remedy for the evil. The government at first refused to interfere, but advised the tulip-holders to agree to some plan among themselves. Several meetings were held for this purpose; but no measure could be devised likely to give satisfaction to the deluded people, or repair even a slight portion of the mischief that had been done. The language of complaint and reproach was in every-body's mouth, and all the meetings were of the most stormy character. At last, however, after much bickering and ill-will, it was agreed, at Amsterdam, by the assem-bled deputies, that all contracts made in the height of the mania, or prior to the month of November 1636, should be declared null and void, and that, in those made after that date, purchasers should be freed from their engage-ments, on paying ten per cent to the vendor. This deci-sion gave no satisfaction. The vendors who had their tulips on hand were, of course, discontented, and those who had pledged themselves to purchase, thought them-selves hardly treated. Tulips which had, at one time, been worth six thousand florins, were now to be procured for five hundred; so that the composition of ten per cent was one hundred florins more than the actual value. Actions for breach of contract were threatened in all the courts of the country; but the latter refused to take cognisance of gambling transactions.

The matter was finally referred to the Provincial Council at the Hague, and it was confidently expected that the wisdom of this body would invent some measure by which credit should be restored. Expectation was on the stretch for its decision, but it never came. The members continued to deliberate week after week, and at last, after thinking about it for three months, declared that they could offer no final decision until they had more information. They advised, however, that, in the mean time, every vendor should, in the presence of witnesses, offer the tulips *in natura* to the purchaser for the sums agreed upon. If the latter refused to take them, they might be put up for sale by public auction, and the original contractor held responsible for the difference between the actual and the stipulated price. This was exactly the plan recommended by the deputies, and which was already shown to be of no avail. There was no court in Holland which would enforce payment. The question was raised in Amsterdam, but the judges unanimously refused to interfere, on the ground that debts contracted in gambling were no debts in law.

Thus the matter rested. To find a remedy was beyond the power of the government. Those who were unlucky enough to have had stores of tulips on hand at the time of the sudden reaction were left to bear their ruin as philosophically as they could; those who had made profits were allowed to keep them; but the commerce of the country suffered a severe shock, from which it was many years ere it recovered.

The example of the Dutch was imitated to some extent in England. In the year 1636 tulips were publicly sold in the Exchange of London, and the jobbers exerted themselves to the utmost to raise them to the fictitious value they had acquired in Amsterdam. In Paris also the jobbers strove to create a tulipomania. In both cities they only partially succeeded. However, the force of example brought the flowers into great favour, and amongst a certain class of people tulips have ever since been prized more highly than any other flowers of the field. The Dutch are still notorious for their partiality to them, and continue to pay higher prices for them than any other people. As the rich Englishman boasts of his fine racehorses or his old pictures, so does the wealthy Dutchman vaunt him of his tulips.

In England, in our day, strange as it may appear, a tulip will produce more money than an oak. If one could be found, *rara in terris*, and black as the black swan alluded to by Juvenal, its price would equal that of a dozen acres of standing corn. In Scotland, towards the close of the seventeenth century, the highest price for tulips, according to the authority of a writer in the supplement to the third edition of the *Encyclopedia Britannica*, was ten guineas. Their value appears to have diminished from that time till the year 1769, when the two most valuable species in England were the Don Quevedo and the Valentinier, the former of which was worth two guineas and the latter two guineas and a half. These prices appear to have been the minimum. In the year 1800, a common price was fifteen guineas for a single bulb. In 1835, so foolish were the fanciers that a bulb of the species called the Miss Fanny Kemble was sold by public auction in London for seventy-five pounds. Still more remarkable was the price of a tulip in the possession of a gardener in the King's Road, Chelsea; in his catalogues it was labelled at two hundred guineas.

4
The Slow Poisoners

PESCARA The like was never read of.
STEPHANO In my judgement,
         To all that shall but hear it, 'twill appear
         A most impossible fable.
PESCARA Troth, I'll tell you,
         And briefly as I can, by what degrees
         They fell into this madness.

Duke of Milan

The atrocious system of poisoning, by poisons so slow in their operation, as to make the victim appear, to ordinary observers, as if dying from a gradual decay of nature, has been practised in all ages. Those who are curious in the matter may refer to Beckmann on Secret Poisons, in his *History of Inventions*, in which he has collected several instances of it from the Greek and Roman writers. Early in the sixteenth century the crime seems to have gradually increased, till, in the seventeenth, it spread over Europe like a pestilence. It was often exercised by pretended witches and sorcerers, and finally became a branch of education amongst all who laid any claim to magical and supernatural arts. In the twenty-first year of Henry VIII an act was passed, rendering it high-treason: those found guilty of it, were to be boiled to death.

One of the first in point of date, and hardly second to any in point of atrocity, is the murder by this means of Sir Thomas Overbury, which disgraced the court of James I, in the year 1613. A slight sketch of it will be a fitting introduction to the history of the poisoning mania, which was so prevalent in France and Italy fifty years later.

Robert Kerr, a Scottish youth, was early taken notice of by James I, and loaded with honours, for no other reason that the world could ever discover than the beauty of his person. James, even in his own day, was suspected of being addicted to the most abominable of all offences, and the more we examine his history now, the stronger the suspicion becomes. However that may be, the handsome Kerr, lending his smooth cheek, even in public, to the disgusting kisses of his royal master, rose rapidly in favour. In the year 1613, he was made Lord High Treasurer of Scotland, and created an English peer, by the style and title of Viscount Rochester. Still further honours were in store for him.

In this rapid promotion he had not been without a friend. Sir Thomas Overbury, the King's secretary – who appears, from some threats in his own letters, to have been no better than a pander to the vices of the King, and privy to his dangerous secrets – exerted all his backstair influence to forward the promotion of Kerr, by whom he was, doubtless, repaid in some way or other. Overbury did not confine his friendship to this, if friendship ever could exist between two such men, but acted the part of an *entremetteur*, and assisted Rochester to carry on an adulterous intrigue with the Lady Frances Howard, the wife of the Earl of Essex. This woman was a person of violent passions, and lost to all sense of shame. Her husband was in her way, and to be freed from him, she instituted proceedings for a divorce, on grounds which a woman of any modesty or delicacy of feeling would die rather than avow. Her scandalous suit was successful, and was no sooner decided than preparations, on a scale of the greatest magnificence, were made for her marriage with Lord Rochester.

Sir Thomas Overbury, who had willingly assisted his patron to intrigue with the Countess of Essex, seems to have imagined that his marriage with so vile a woman might retard his advancement; he accordingly employed all his influence to dissuade him from it. But Rochester was bent on the match, and his passions were as violent as those of the Countess. On one occasion, when Overbury and the Viscount were walking in the gallery of Whitehall, Overbury was overheard to say, 'Well, my Lord, if you do marry that base woman, you will utterly ruin your honour and yourself. You shall never do it with my advice or consent; and, if you do, you had best look to stand fast.' Rochester flung from him in a rage, exclaiming with an oath, 'I will be even with you for this.' These words were the death-warrant of the unfortunate Overbury. He had mortally wounded the pride of Rochester in insinuating that by his (Overbury's) means he might be lowered in the King's favour; and he had endeavoured to curb the burning passions of a heartless, dissolute, and reckless man.

Overbury's imprudent remonstrances were reported to the Countess; and from that moment, she also vowed the most deadly vengeance against him. With a fiendish hypocrisy, however, they both concealed their intentions, and Overbury, at the solicitation of Rochester, was appointed ambassador to the court of Russia. This apparent favour was but the first step in a deep and deadly plot. Rochester, pretending to be warmly attached to the interests of Overbury, advised him to refuse the embassy, which, he said, was but a trick to get him out of the way. He promised, at the same time, to stand between him and any evil consequences which might result from his refusal. Overbury fell into the snare, and declined the embassy. James, offended, immediately ordered his committal to the Tower.

He was now in safe custody, and his enemies had opportunity to commence the work of vengeance. The first thing Rochester did was to procure, by his influence at court, the dismissal of the Lieutenant of the Tower, and the appointment of Sir Jervis Elwes, one of his creatures, to the vacant post. This man was but one instrument, and another being necessary, was found in Richard Weston, a fellow who had formerly been shopman to a druggist. He was installed in the office of under-keeper, and as such had the direct custody of Overbury. So far, all was favourable to the designs of the conspirators.

In the mean time, the insidious Rochester wrote the most friendly letters to Overbury, requesting him to bear his ill-fortune patiently, and promising that his imprisonment should not be of long duration; for that his friends were exerting themselves to soften the King's displeasure. Still pretending the extreme of sympathy for him, he followed up the letters by presents of pastry and other delicacies, which could not be procured in the Tower.

These articles were all poisoned. Occasionally, presents of a similar description were sent to Sir Jervis Elwes, with the understanding that these articles were not poisoned, when they were unaccompanied by letters: of these the unfortunate prisoner never tasted. A woman, named Turner, who had formerly kept a house of ill fame, and who had more than once lent it to further the guilty intercourse of Rochester and Lady Essex, was the agent employed to procure the poisons. They were prepared by Dr Forman, a pretended fortune-teller of Lambeth, assisted by an apothecary named Franklin. Both these persons knew for what purposes the poisons were needed, and employed their skill in mixing them in the pastry and other edibles, in such small quantities as gradually to wear out the constitution of their victim. Mrs Turner regularly furnished the poisoned articles to the under-keeper, who placed them before Overbury. Not only his food, but his drink was poisoned. Arsenic was mixed with the salt he ate, and cantharides with the pepper. All this time, his health declined sensibly. Every day he grew weaker and weaker; and with a sickly appetite, craved for sweets and jellies. Rochester continued to condole with him, and anticipated all his wants in this respect, sending him abundance of pastry, and occasionally partridges and other game, and young pigs. With the sauce for the game, Mrs Turner mixed a quantity of cantharides, and poisoned the pork with lunar-caustic. As stated on the trial, Overbury took in this manner poison enough to have poisoned twenty men; but his constitution was strong, and he still lingered. Franklin, the apothecary, confessed that he prepared with Dr Forman seven different sorts of poisons; viz. aquafortis, arsenic, mercury, powder of diamonds, lunar-caustic, great spiders, and cantharides. Overbury held out so long that Rochester became impatient, and in a letter to Lady Essex, expressed his wonder that things were not sooner despatched. Orders were immediately sent by Lady Essex to the keeper to finish with the victim at once. Overbury had not been all this time without suspicion of treachery, although he appears to have had no idea of poison. He merely suspected that it was intended to confine him for life, and to set the King still more bitterly against him. In one of his letters, he threatened Rochester that, unless he were speedily liberated, he would expose his villainy to the world. He says, 'You and I, ere it be long, will come to a public trial of another nature . . . Drive me not to extremities, lest I should say something that both you and I should repent . . . Whether I live or die, your shame shall never die, but ever remain to the world, to make you the most odious man living . . . I wonder much you should neglect him to whom such secrets of all kinds have passed . . . Be these the fruits of common secrets, common dangers?'

All these remonstrances, and hints as to the dangerous secrets in his keeping, were ill-calculated to serve him with a man so reckless as Lord Rochester: they were more likely to cause him to be sacrificed than to be saved. Rochester appears to have acted as if he thought so. He doubtless employed the murderer's reasoning that 'dead men tell no tales', when, after receiving letters of this description, he complained to his paramour of the delay. Weston was spurred on to consummate the atrocity; and the patience of all parties being exhausted, a dose of corrosive sublimate was administered to him, in October 1613, which put an end to his sufferings, after he had been for six months in their hands. On the very day of his death, and before his body was cold, he was wrapped up carelessly in a sheet, and buried without any funeral ceremony in a pit within the precincts of the Tower.

Sir Anthony Weldon, in his *Court and Character of James I*, gives a somewhat different account of the closing scene of this tragedy. He says, 'Franklin and Weston came into Overbury's chamber, and found him in infinite torment, with contention between the strength of nature and the working of the poison; and it being very like that nature had gotten the better in this contention, by the thrusting out of boils, blotches, and blains, they, fearing it might come to light by the judgement of physicians, the foul play that had been offered him, consented to stifle him with the bedclothes, which accordingly was performed; and so ended his miserable life, with the assurance of the conspirators that he died by the poison; none thinking otherwise than these two murderers.'

The sudden death – the indecent haste of the funeral, and the non-holding of an inquest upon the body, strengthened the suspicions that were afloat. Rumour, instead of whispering, began to speak out; and the relatives of the deceased openly expressed their belief that their kinsman had been murdered. But Rochester was still all powerful at court, and no one dared to utter a word to his discredit. Shortly afterwards, his marriage with the Countess of Essex was celebrated with the utmost splendour, the King himself being present at the ceremony.

It would seem that Overbury's knowledge of James's character was deeper than Rochester had given him credit for, and that he had been a true prophet when he predicted that his marriage would eventually estrange James from his minion. At this time, however, Rochester stood higher than ever in the royal favour; but it did not last long – conscience, that busy monitor, was at work. The tongue of rumour was never still; and Rochester, who had long been a guilty, became at last a wretched man. His cheeks lost their colour – his eyes grew dim; and he became moody, careless, and melancholy. The King seeing him thus, took at length no pleasure in his society, and began to look about for another favourite. George Villiers, Duke of Buckingham, was the man to his mind; quickwitted, handsome, and unscrupulous. The two latter qualities alone were sufficient to recommend him to James I. In proportion as the influence of Rochester declined, that of Buckingham increased. A falling favourite has no friends; and Rumour wagged her tongue against Rochester louder and more pertinaciously than ever. A new favourite, too, generally endeavours to hasten by a kick the fall of the old one; and Buckingham, anxious to work the complete ruin of his forerunner in the King's good graces, encouraged the relatives of Sir Thomas Overbury to prosecute their enquiries into the strange death of their kinsman.

James was rigorous enough in the punishment of offences when he was not himself involved. He piqued himself, moreover, on his dexterity in unravelling mysteries. The affair of Sir Thomas Overbury found him congenial occupation. He set to work by ordering the arrest of Sir Jervis Elwes. James, at this early stage of the proceedings, does not seem to have been aware that Rochester was so deeply implicated. Struck with horror at the atrocious system of slow poisoning, the King sent for all the Judges. According to Sir Anthony Weldon, he knelt down in the midst of them, and said, 'My Lords the Judges, it is lately come to my hearing that you have now in examination a business of poisoning. Lord! in what a miserable condition shall this kingdom be (the only famous nation for hospitality in the world) if our tables should become such a snare, as that none could eat without danger of life, and that Italian custom should be introduced among us! Therefore, my Lords, I charge you, as you will answer it at that great and dreadful day of judgement, that you examine it strictly, without layout, affection, or partiality. And if you shall spare any guilty of this crime, God's curse light on you and your posterity! and if I spare any that are guilty, God's curse light on me and my posterity for ever!'

The imprecation fell but too surely upon the devoted house of Stuart. The solemn oath was broken, and God's curse did light upon him and his posterity!

The next person arrested after Sir Jervis Elwes, was Weston, the under-keeper; then Franklin and Mrs Turner; and, lastly, the Earl and Countess of Somerset, to which dignity Rochester had been advanced since the death of Overbury.

Weston was first brought to trial. Public curiosity was on the stretch. Nothing else was talked of, and the court on the day of trial was crowded to suffocation. The State Trials report, that Lord Chief Justice Coke 'laid open to the jury the baseness and cowardliness of poisoners, who attempt that secretly against which there is no means of preservation or defence for a man's life; and how rare it was to hear of any poisoning in England, so detestable it was to our nation. But the devil had taught divers to be cunning in it, so that they can poison in what distance of space they please, by consuming the *nativum calidum*, or *humidum radicale*, in one month, two or three, or more, as they list, which they four manner of ways do execute; viz. 'Haustu', 'gustu', 'odore', and 'contactu'.

When the indictment was read over, Weston made no other reply than, 'Lord have mercy upon me! Lord have mercy upon me!' On being asked how he would be tried, he refused to throw himself upon a jury of his country, and declared, that he would be tried by God alone. In this he persisted for some time. The fear of the dreadful punishment for contumacy* induced him, at length, to plead 'Not guilty', and take his trial in due course of law.

---

* The punishment for the contumacious was expressed by the words *onere, frigore, et fame*. By the first was meant that the culprit should be extended on his back on the ground, and weights placed over his body, gradually increased, until he expired. Sometimes the punishment was not extended to this length, and the victim, being allowed to recover, underwent the second portion, the *frigore*, which consisted in his standing naked in the open air, for a certain space, in the sight of all the people. The third, or *fame*, was more dreadful, the statute saying, 'That he was to be preserved with the coarsest bread that could be got, and water out of the next sink or puddle, to the place of execution; and that day he had water he should have no bread, and that day he had bread, he should have no water'; and in this torment he was to linger as long as nature would hold out.

All the circumstances against him were fully proved, and he was found guilty and executed at Tyburn. Mrs Turner, Franklin, and Sir Jervis Elwes were also brought to trial, found guilty, and executed between the 19th of October and the 4th of December 1615; but the grand trial of the Earl and Countess of Somerset did not take place till the month of May following.

On the trial of Sir Jervis Elwes, circumstances had transpired, showing a guilty knowledge of the poisoning on the part of the Earl of Northampton the uncle of Lady Somerset, and the chief falconer Sir Thomas Monson. The former was dead; but Sir Thomas Monson was arrested, and brought to trial. It appeared, however, that he was too dangerous a man to be brought to the scaffold. He knew too many of the odious secrets of James I, and his dying speech might contain disclosures which would compromise the King. To conceal old guilt it was necessary to incur new: the trial of Sir Thomas Monson was brought to an abrupt conclusion, and himself set at liberty!

Already James had broken his oath: He now began to fear that he had been rash in engaging so zealously to bring the poisoners to punishment. That Somerset would be declared guilty there was no doubt, and that he looked for pardon and impunity was equally evident to the King. Somerset, while in the Tower, asserted confidently, that James would not *dare* to bring him to trial. In this he was mistaken; but James was in an agony. What the secret was between them will now never be known with certainty; but it may be surmised. Some have imagined it to be the vice to which the King was addicted; while others have asserted, that it related to the death of Prince Henry, a virtuous young man, who had held Somerset in especial abhorrence. The Prince died early, unlamented by his father, and, as public opinion whispered at the time, poisoned by Somerset. Probably, some crime or other lay heavy upon the soul of the King; and Somerset, his accomplice, could not be brought to public execution with safety. Hence the dreadful tortures of James, when he discovered that his favourite was so deeply implicated in the murder of Overbury. Every means was taken by the agonised King to bring the prisoner into what was called a safe frame of mind. He was secretly advised to plead guilty, and trust to the clemency of the King. The same advice was conveyed to the Countess. Bacon was instructed by the King to draw up a paper of all the points of 'mercy and favour' to Somerset which might result from the evidence; and Somerset was again recommended to plead guilty, and promised that no evil should ensue to him.

The Countess was first tried. She trembled and shed tears during the reading of the indictment, and, in a low voice, pleaded guilty. On being asked why sentence of death should not be passed against her, she replied meekly, 'I can much aggravate, but nothing extenuate my fault. I desire mercy, and that the lords will intercede for me with the King.' Sentence of death was passed upon her.

Next day the Earl was brought to trial. He appears to have mistrusted the promises of James, and he pleaded not guilty. With a self-possession and confidence, which he felt, probably, from his knowledge of the King's character, he rigorously cross-examined the witnesses, and made a stubborn defence. After a trial which lasted eleven hours, he was found guilty, and condemned to the felon's death.

Whatever may have been the secrets between the criminal and the King, the latter, notwithstanding his terrific oath, was afraid to sign the death-warrant. It might, perchance, have been his own. The Earl and Countess were committed to the Tower, where they remained for nearly five years. At the end of this period, to the surprise and scandal of the community, and the disgrace of its chief magistrate, they both received the royal pardon, but were ordered to reside at a distance from the court. Having been found guilty of felony, the estates of the Earl had become forfeited; but James granted him out of their revenues an income of £4,000 per annum! Shamelessness could go no further.

Of the after life of these criminals nothing is known, except that the love they had formerly borne each other was changed into aversion, and that they lived under the same roof for months together without the interchange of a word.

The exposure of their atrocities did not put a stop to the practice of poisoning. On the contrary, as we shall see hereafter, it engendered that insane imitation which is so strange a feature of the human character. James himself is supposed, with great probability, to have fallen a victim to it. In the notes to Harris's *Life and Writings of James I*, there is a good deal of information on the subject. The guilt of Buckingham, although not fully established, rests upon circumstances of suspicion stronger than have been sufficient to lead hundreds to the scaffold. His motives for committing the crime are stated to have been a desire of revenge for the coldness with which the King, in the latter years of his reign, began to regard him; his fear that James intended to degrade him; and his hope that the great influence he possessed over the mind of the heir-apparent would last through a new reign, if the old one were brought to a close.

In the second volume of the *Harleian Miscellany*, there is a tract, entitled the 'Forerunner of Revenge', written by George Eglisham, doctor of medicine, and one of the physicians to King James. Harris, in quoting it, says that it is full of rancour and prejudice. It is evidently exaggerated; but forms, nevertheless, a link in the chain of evidence. Eglisham says: 'The King being sick of an ague, the Duke took this opportunity, when all the King's doctors of physic were at dinner, and offered to him a white powder to take, the which he a long time refused; but, overcome with his flattering importunity, he took it in wine, and immediately became worse and worse, falling into many swoonings and pains, and violent fluxes of the belly, so tormented, that his Majesty cried out aloud of this white powder, "Would to God I had never taken it!"' He then tells us 'of the Countess of Buckingham (the Duke's mother) applying the plaister to the King's heart and breast, whereupon he grew faint and short-breathed, and in agony. That the physicians exclaimed, that the King was poisoned; that Buckingham commanded them out of the room, and committed one of them close prisoner to his own chamber, and another to be removed from court; and that, after his Majesty's death, his body and head swelled above measure; his hair, with the skin of his head, stuck to his pillow, and his nails became loose on his fingers and toes.' Clarendon, who, by the way, was a partisan of the Duke's, gives a totally different account of James's death. He says, 'It was occasioned by an ague (after a short indisposition by the gout) which, meeting many humours in a fat unwieldy body of fifty-eight years old, in four or five fits carried him out of the world. After whose death many scandalous and libellous discourses were raised, without the least colour or ground; as appeared upon the strictest and most malicious examination that could be made, long after, in a time of licence, when nobody was afraid of offending majesty, and when prosecuting the highest reproaches and contumelies against the royal family was held very meritorious.' Notwithstanding this confident declaration, the world will hardly be persuaded that there was not some truth in the rumours that were abroad. The enquiries which were instituted were not strict, as he asserts, and all the unconstitutional influence of the powerful favourite was exerted to defeat them. In the celebrated accusations brought against Buckingham by the Earl of Bristol, the poisoning of King James was placed last on the list, and the pages of history bear evidence of the summary mode in which they were, for the time, got rid of.

The man from whom Buckingham is said to have procured his poisons was one Dr Lamb, a conjuror and empiric, who, besides dealing in poisons, pretended to be a fortune-teller. The popular fury, which broke with comparative harmlessness against his patron, was directed against this man, until he could not appear with safety in the streets of London. His fate was melancholy. Walking one day in Cheapside, disguised, as he thought, from all observers, he was recognised by some idle boys, who began to hoot and pelt him with rubbish, calling out, 'The poisoner! the poisoner! Down with the wizard! down with him!' A mob very soon collected, and the Doctor took to his heels and ran for his life. He was pursued and seized in Wood Street, and from thence dragged by the hair through the mire to St Paul's Cross; the mob beating him with sticks and stones, and calling out, 'Kill the wizard! kill the poisoner!'

Charles I, on hearing of the riot, rode from Whitehall to quell it; but he arrived too late to save the victim. Every bone in his body was broken, and he was quite dead. Charles was excessively indignant, and fined the city six hundred pounds for its inability to deliver up the ringleaders to justice.

But it was in Italy that poisoning was most prevalent. From a very early period, it seems to have been looked upon in that country as a perfectly justifiable means of getting rid of an enemy. The Italians of the sixteenth and seventeenth centuries poisoned their opponents with as little compunction as an Englishman of the present day brings an action at law against anyone who has done him an injury. The writings of contemporary authors inform us that, when La Spara and La Tophania carried on their infernal trade, ladies put poison bottles on their dressing-tables as openly, and used them with as little scruple upon others, as modern dames use *Eau de Cologne* or lavender-water upon themselves. So powerful is the influence of fashion, it can even cause murder to be regarded as a venial peccadillo. In the memoirs of the last Duke of Guise, who made a Quixotic attempt, in 1648, to seize upon the government of Naples, we find some curious particulars relative to the popular feeling with regard to poisoning. A man, named Gennaro Annese, who, after the short and extraordinary career of Masaniello the fisherman, had established himself as a sort of captain-general of the populace, rendered himself so obnoxious to the Duke of Guise that the adherents of the latter determined to murder him. The captain of the guard, as the Duke himself very coolly informs us, was requested to undertake this office. It was suggested to him that the *poniard* would be the most effectual instrument, but the man turned up his eyes with pious horror at the proposition. He was ready to poison Gennaro Annese whenever he might be called upon to do so; but to poniard him, he said, would be disgraceful, and unbecoming an officer of the guards! At last *poison* was agreed upon, and Augustino Molla, an attorney in the Duke's confidence, brought the bottle containing the liquid to show it to his master. The following is the Duke's own account:

Augustino came to me at night, and told me: 'I have brought you something which will free you from Gennaro. He deserves death, and it is no great matter after what fashion justice is done upon him. Look at this vial, full of clear and beautiful water: in four days' time, it will punish all his treasons. The captain of the guard has undertaken to give it him; and as it has no taste at all, Gennaro will suspect nothing.'

The Duke further informs us that the dose was duly administered; but that Gennaro, fortunately for himself, ate nothing for dinner that day but cabbage dressed with oil, which, acting as an antidote, caused him to vomit profusely, and saved his life. He was exceedingly ill for five days, but never suspected that he had been poisoned.

In process of time, poison vending became a profitable trade. Eleven years after this period, it was carried on at Rome to such an extent that the sluggish government was roused to interference. Beckmann, in his *History of Inventions*, and Lebret, in his *Magazin zum Gebrauche der Staaten Kirche Geschichte*, or Magazine of Materials for a History of a State Church, relates that, in the year 1659, it was made known to Pope Alexander VII that great numbers of young women had avowed in the confessional that they had poisoned their husbands with slow poisons. The Catholic clergy, who in general hold the secrets of the confessional so sacred, were shocked and alarmed at the extraordinary prevalence of the crime. Although they refrained from revealing the names of the penitents, they conceived themselves bound to apprise the head of the Church of the enormities that were practised. It was also the subject of general conversation in Rome that young widows were unusually abundant. It was remarked, too, that if any couple lived unhappily together, the husband soon took ill and died. The papal authorities, when once they began to enquire, soon learned that a society of young wives had been formed, and met nightly, for some mysterious purpose, at the house of an old woman named Hieronyma Spara. This hag was a reputed witch and fortune-teller, and acted as president of the young viragos, several of whom, it was afterwards ascertained, belonged to the first families of Rome.

In order to have positive evidence of the practices of this female conclave, a lady was employed by the Government to seek an interview with them. She dressed herself out in the most magnificent style; and having been amply provided with money, she found but little difficulty, when she had stated her object, of procuring an audience of La Spara and her sisterhood. She pretended to be in extreme distress of mind on account of the infidelities and ill-treatment of her husband, and implored La Spara to furnish her with a few drops of the wonderful elixir, the efficacy of which in sending cruel husbands to 'their last long sleep' was so much vaunted by the ladies of Rome. La Spara fell into the snare, and sold her some of her 'drops', at a price commensurate with the supposed wealth of the purchaser.

The liquor thus obtained was subjected to an analysis, and found to be, as was suspected, a slow poison – clear, tasteless, and limpid, like that spoken of by the Duke of Guise. Upon this evidence the house was surrounded by the police, and La Spara and her companions taken into custody. La Spara, who is described as having been a little, ugly, old woman, was put to the torture, but obstinately refused to confess her guilt. Another of the women, named La Gratiosa, had less firmness, and laid bare all the secrets of the infernal sisterhood. Taking a confession, extorted by anguish on the rack, at its true value (nothing at all), there is still sufficient evidence to warrant posterity in the belief of their guilt. They were found guilty, and condemned, according to their degrees of culpability, to various punishments. La Spara, Gratiosa, and three young women, who had poisoned their husbands, were hanged

together at Rome. Upwards of thirty women were whipped publicly through the streets; and several, whose high
rank screened them from more degrading punishment,
were banished from the country, and mulcted in heavy
fines. In a few months afterwards, nine women more
were hanged for poisoning; and another bevy, including
many young and beautiful girls, were whipped half naked
through the streets of Rome.

This severity did not put a stop to the practice, and jeal-
ous women and avaricious men, anxious to step into the
inheritance of fathers, uncles, or brothers, resorted to poison. As it was quite free from taste, colour, and smell, it
was administered without exciting suspicion. The skilful
vendors compounded it of different degrees of strength,
so that the poisoners had only to say whether they wanted
their victims to die in a week, a month, or six months, and
they were suited with corresponding doses. The vendors
were chiefly women, of whom the most celebrated was a
hag, named Tophania, who was in this way accessory to
the death of upwards of six hundred persons. This woman
appears to have been a dealer in poisons from her girl-
hood, and resided first at Palermo and then at Naples.
That entertaining traveller, Father Lebat, has given, in his
Letters from Italy, many curious particulars relating to
her. When he was at Civita Vecchia, in 1719, the Viceroy of
Naples discovered that poison was extensively sold in the
latter city, and that it went by the name of *aqueta*, or little-
water. On making further enquiry, he ascertained that
Tophania (who was by this time near seventy years of age,
and who seems to have begun her evil courses very soon
after the execution of La Spara) sent large quantities of it

to all parts of Italy in small vials, with the inscription 'Manna of St Nicholas of Barri'.

The tomb of St Nicholas of Barri was celebrated throughout Italy. A miraculous oil was said to ooze from it, which cured nearly all the maladies that flesh is heir to, provided the recipient made use of it with the due degree of faith. La Tophania artfully gave this name to her poison to elude the vigilance of the custom-house officers, who, in common with everybody else, had a pious respect for St Nicholas de Barri and his wonderful oil.

The poison was similar to that manufactured by La Spara. Hahnemann the physician, and father of the homoeopathic doctrine, writing upon this subject, says it was compounded of arsenical neutral salts, occasioning in the victim a gradual loss of appetite, faintness, gnawing pains in the stomach, loss of strength, and wasting of the lungs. The Abbé Gagliardi says that a few drops of it were generally poured into tea, chocolate, or soup, and its effects were slow, and almost imperceptible. Garelli, physician to the Emperor of Austria, in a letter to Hoffmann, says it was crystallised arsenic, dissolved in a large quantity of water by decoction, with the addition (for some unexplained purpose) of the herb cymbalaria. The Neapolitans called it *Aqua Toffnina*; and it became notorious all over Europe under the name of *Aqua Tophania*.

Although this woman carried on her infamous traffic so extensively, it was extremely difficult to meet with her. She lived in continual dread of discovery. She constantly changed her name and residence; and pretending to be a person of great godliness, resided in monasteries for months together. Whenever she was more than usually apprehensive of detection, she sought ecclesiastical protection. She was soon apprised of the search made for her by the Viceroy of Naples, and, according to her practice, took refuge in a monastery. Either the search after her was not very rigid, or her measures were exceedingly well taken; for she contrived to elude the vigilance of the authorities for several years. What is still more extraordinary, as showing the ramifications of her system, her trade was still carried on to as great an extent as before. Lebat informs us that she had so great a sympathy for poor wives who hated their husbands and wanted to get rid of them, but could not afford to buy her wonderful *aqua*, that she made them presents of it.

She was not allowed, however, to play at this game for ever; she was at length discovered in a nunnery, and her retreat cut off. The Viceroy made several representations to the superior to deliver her up, but without effect. The abbess, supported by the archbishop of the diocese, constantly refused. The public curiosity was in consequence so much excited at the additional importance thus thrust upon the criminal, that thousands of persons visited the nunnery in order to catch a glimpse of her.

The patience of the Viceroy appears to have been exhausted by these delays. Being a man of sense, and not a very zealous Catholic, he determined that even the Church should not shield a criminal so atrocious. Setting the privileges of the nunnery at defiance, he sent a troop of soldiers, who broke over the walls and carried her away *vi et armis*. The Archbishop, Cardinal Pignatelli, was highly indignant, and threatened to excommunicate and lay the whole city under interdict. All the inferior clergy, animated by the *esprit du corps*, took up the question, and so worked upon the superstitious and bigoted people, that they were ready to rise in a mass to storm the palace of the Viceroy and rescue the prisoner.

These were serious difficulties; but the Viceroy was not a man to be daunted. Indeed, he seems to have acted throughout with a rare union of astuteness, coolness, and energy. To avoid the evil consequences of the threatened excommunication, he placed a guard round the palace of the Archbishop, judging that the latter would not be so foolish as to launch out an anathema which would cause the city to be starved, and himself in it. The market-people would not have dared to come to the city with provisions, so long as it remained under the ban. There would have been too much inconvenience to himself and his ghostly brethren in such a measure; and, as the Viceroy anticipated, the good Cardinal reserved his thunders for some other occasion.

Still there was the populace. To quiet their clamour and avert the impending insurrection, the agents of the government adroitly mingled with the people, and spread abroad a report that Tophania had poisoned all the wells and fountains of the city. This was enough. The popular feeling turned against her immediately. Those who, but a moment before, had looked upon her as a saint, now reviled her as a devil, and were as eager for her punishment as they had before been for her escape. Tophania was then put to the torture. She confessed the long catalogue of her crimes, and named all the persons who had employed her. She was shortly afterwards strangled, and her corpse thrown over the wall into the garden of the convent, from whence she had been taken. This appears to have been done to conciliate the clergy, by allowing them, at least, the burial of one who had taken refuge within their precincts.

After her death the mania for poisoning seems to have abated; but we have yet to see what hold it took upon the French people at a somewhat earlier period. So rooted had it become in France between the years 1670 and 1680, that Mme de Sévigné, in one of her letters, expresses her fear that Frenchman and poisoner would become synonymous terms.

As in Italy, the first notice the government received of the prevalence of this crime was given by the clergy, to whom females of high rank, and some among the middle and lower classes, had avowed in the confessional that they had poisoned their husbands. In consequence of these disclosures, two Italians, named Exili and Glaser, were arrested, and thrown into the Bastille, on the charge of compounding and selling the drugs used for these murders. Glaser died in prison, but Exili remained without trial for several months; and there, shortly afterwards, he made the acquaintance of another prisoner, named Sainte Croix, by whose example the crime was still further disseminated among the French people.

The most notorious of the poisoners that derived their pernicious knowledge from this man was Mme de Brinvilliers, a young woman connected both by birth and marriage with some of the noblest families of France. She seems, from her very earliest years, to have been heartless and depraved; and, if we may believe her own confession, was steeped in wickedness ere she had well entered her teens. She was, however, beautiful and accomplished; and, in the eye of the world, seemed exemplary and kind. Guyot de Pitaval, in the *Causes Célèbres*, and Mme de Sévigné, in her *Letters*, represent her as mild and agreeable in her manners, and offering no traces on her countenance of the evil soul within. She was married in 1651 to the Marquis de Brinvilliers, with whom she lived unhappily for some years. He was a loose, dissipated character, and was the means of introducing Sainte Croix to his wife, a man who cast a blight upon her life, and dragged her on from crime to crime till her offences became so great that the mind shudders to dwell upon them. For this man she conceived a guilty passion, to gratify which she plunged at once into the gulf of sin. She was drawn to its most loathsome depths ere retribution overtook her.

She had as yet shown a fair outside to the world, and found but little difficulty in effecting a legal separation from her husband, who had not the art to conceal his vices. The proceeding gave great offence to her family. She appears, after this, to have thrown off the mask completely, and carried on her intrigues so openly with her lover, Sainte Croix, that her father, M. D'Aubray, scandalised at her conduct, procured a *lettre de cachet*, and had him imprisoned in the Bastille for a twelvemonth.

Sainte Croix, who had been in Italy, was a dabbler in poisons. He knew something of the secrets of the detestable La Spara, and improved himself in them from the instructions of Exili, with whom he speedily contracted a sort of friendship. By him he was shown how to prepare, not only the liquid poisons employed in Italy, but that known as succession powder, which afterwards became so celebrated in France. Like his mistress, he appeared amiable, witty, and intelligent, and showed no signs to the world of the two fierce passions, revenge and avarice, which were gnawing at his heart. Both these passions were to be sated on the unfortunate family of D'Aubray; his revenge, because they had imprisoned him; and his avarice, because they were rich. Reckless and extravagant, he was always in want of money, and he had no one to supply him but Mme de Brinvilliers, whose own portion was far from sufficient to satisfy his need. Groaning to think that any impediment should stand between him and wealth, he conceived the horrid idea of poisoning M. D'Aubray her father, and her two brothers, that she might inherit the property. Three murders were nothing to such a villain. He communicated his plan to Mme de Brinvilliers; and she, without the slightest scruple, agreed to aid him: he undertook to compound the poisons, and she to administer them. The zeal and alacrity with which she set to work seem hardly credible. Sainte Croix found her an apt scholar; and she soon became as expert as himself in the manufacture of poisons. To try the strength of the first doses, she used to administer them to dogs, rabbits, and pigeons. Afterwards, wishing to be more certain of their effects, she went round to the hospitals, and administered them to the sick poor in the soups which she brought in apparent charity. None of the poisons were intended to kill at the first dose; so that she could try them once upon an individual without fear of murder. She tried the same atrocious experiment upon the guests at her father's table, by poisoning a pigeon-pie! To be more certain still, she next poisoned herself! When convinced by this desperate essay of the potency of the draught, she procured an antidote from Sainte Croix, and all doubts being removed, commenced operations upon her grey-headed father. She administered the first dose with her own hands, in his chocolate. The poison worked well. The old man was taken ill, and his daughter, apparently full of tenderness and anxiety, watched by his bedside. The next day she gave him some broth, which she recommended as highly nourishing. This also was poisoned. In this manner she gradually wore out his frame, and in less than ten days he was a corpse! His death seemed so much the result of disease, that no suspicions were excited.

When the two brothers arrived from the provinces to render the last sad duties to their sire, they found their sister as grieved, to all outward appearance, as even filial affection could desire: but the young men only came to perish. They stood between Sainte Croix and the already half-clutched gold, and their doom was sealed. A man, named La Chaussée, was hired by Sainte Croix to aid in administering the poisons; and, in less than six weeks' time, they had both gone to their long home.

Suspicion was now excited; but so cautiously had all been done, that it found no one upon whom to attach itself. The Marquise had a sister, and she was entitled, by the death of her relatives, to half the property. Less than the whole would not satisfy Sainte Croix, and he determined that she should die the same death as her father and brothers. She was too distrustful, however; and, by quitting Paris, she escaped the destruction that was lurking for her.

The Marquise had undertaken these murders to please her lover. She was now anxious to perpetrate another on her own account. She wished to marry Sainte Croix; but, though separated from her husband, she was not divorced. She thought it would be easier to poison him than to apply to the tribunals for a divorce, which might, perhaps, be refused. But Sainte Croix had no longer any love for his guilty instrument. Bad men do not admire others who are as bad as themselves. Though a villain himself, he had no desire to marry one, and was not at all anxious for the death of the Marquis. He seemed, however, to enter into the plot, and supplied her with poison for her husband: but he took care to provide a remedy. La Brinvilliers poisoned him one day, and Sainte Croix gave him an antidote the next. In this manner he was buffetted about between them for some time, and finally escaped with a ruined constitution and a broken heart.

But the day of retribution was at hand, and a terrible mischance brought the murders to light. The nature of the poisons compounded by Sainte Croix was so deadly, that, when working in his laboratory, he was obliged to wear a mask, to preserve himself from suffocation. One day, the mask slipped off, and the miserable wretch perished in his crimes. His corpse was found, on the following morning, in the obscure lodging where he had fitted up his laboratory. As he appeared to be without friends or relatives, the police took possession of his effects. Among other things was found a small box, to which was affixed the following singular document:

I humbly beg, that those into whose hands this box may fall, will do me the favour to deliver it into the hands only of the Marchioness de Brinvilliers, who resides in the Rue Neuve St Paul, as everything it contains concerns her, and belongs to her alone; and as, besides, there is nothing in it that can be of use to any person but her. In case she shall be dead before me, it is my wish that it be burned, with everything it contains, without opening or altering anything. In order that no one may plead ignorance, I swear by the God that I adore, and by all that is held most sacred, that I assert nothing but the truth: and if my intentions, just and reasonable as they are, be thwarted in this point by any persons, I charge their consciences with it, both in this world and that which is to come, in order that I may unload mine. I protest that this is my last will. Done at Paris, the 25th of May, 1672.

(Signed) Sainte Croix

This earnest solicitation, instead of insuring respect as was intended, excited curiosity. The box was opened, and found to contain some papers, and several vials and powders. The latter were handed to a chemist for analysis, and the documents were retained by the police, and opened. Among them was found a promissory note of the Marchioness de Brinvilliers, for thirty thousand francs, to the order of Sainte Croix. The other papers were of greater importance, as they implicated both her and her servant, La Chaussée, in the recent murders. As soon as she was informed of the death of Sainte Croix, she made an attempt to gain possession of his papers and the box; but, being refused, she saw that there was no time to be lost, and immediately quitted. Next morning the police were on her trail; but she succeeded in escaping to England. La Chaussée was not so fortunate. Altogether ignorant of the fatal mischance which had brought his villainies to light, he did not dream of danger. He was arrested and brought to trial: being put to the torture, he confessed that he had administered poison to the Messieurs d'Aubray, and that he had received a hundred pistoles, and the promise of an annuity for life, from Sainte Croix and Mme de Brinvilliers, for the job. He was condemned to be broken alive on the wheel, and the Marchioness was, by default, sentenced to be beheaded. He was executed accordingly, in March 1673, on the Place de Grève, in Paris.

La Brinvilliers appears to have resided for nearly three years in England. Early in 1676, thinking that the rigour of pursuit was over, and that she might venture to return to the Continent, she proceeded secretly to Liège. Notwithstanding her care, the French authorities were soon apprised of her return; and arrangements were promptly made with the municipality of that city, to permit the agents of the French police to arrest her within the limits of their jurisdiction. Desgrais, an officer of the Maréchausée, accordingly left Paris for that purpose. On his arrival in Liège, he found that she had sought shelter within the walls of a convent. Here the arm of the law, long as it is said to be, could not reach her: but Desgrais was not a man to be baffled, and he resorted to stratagem to accomplish what force could not. Having disguised himself as a priest, he sought admission to the convent, and obtained an interview with La Brinvilliers. He said, that being a Frenchman, and passing through Liège, he could not leave that city without paying a visit to a lady whose beauty and misfortunes were so celebrated. Her vanity was flattered by the compliment. Desgrais saw, to use a vulgar but forcible expression, 'that he had got on the blind side of her'; and he adroitly continued to pour out the language of love and admiration, till the deluded Marchioness was thrown completely off her guard. She agreed, without much solicitation, to meet him outside the walls of the convent, where their amorous intrigue might be carried on more conveniently than within. Faithful to her appointment with her supposed new lover, she came, and found herself, not in the embrace of a gallant, but in the custody of a policeman.

Her trial was not long delayed. The proofs against her were abundant. The dying declaration of La Chaussée would have been alone enough to convict her; but besides that, there were the mysterious document attached to the box of St Croix; her flight from France; and, stronger and more damning proof than all, a paper, in her own handwriting, found among the effects of St Croix, in which she detailed to him the misdeeds of her life, and spoke of the murder of her father and brothers, in terms that left no doubt of her guilt. During the trial, all Paris was in commotion. La Brinvilliers was the only subject of conversation. All the details of her crimes were published, and greedily devoured; and the idea of secret poisoning was first put into the heads of hundreds, who afterwards became guilty of it.

On the 16th of July 1676, the Superior Criminal Court of Paris pronounced a verdict of guilty against her, for the murder of her father and brothers, and the attempt upon the life of her sister. She was condemned to be drawn on a hurdle, with her feet bare, a rope about her neck, and a burning torch in her hand, to the great entrance of the cathedral of Notre Dame; where she was to make the *amende honorable*, in sight of all the people; to be taken from thence to the Place de Grève, and there to be beheaded. Her body was afterwards to be burned, and her ashes scattered to the winds.

After her sentence, she made a full confession of her guilt. She seems to have looked upon death without fear; but it was recklessness, not courage, that supported her. Mme de Sévigné says, that when on the hurdle, on her way to the scaffold, she entreated her confessor to exert his influence with the executioner to place himself next to her, that his body might hide from her view 'that scoundrel, Desgrais, who had entrapped her'. She also asked the ladies, who had been drawn to their windows to witness the procession, what they were looking at? adding, 'a pretty sight you have come to see, truly!' She laughed when on the scaffold, dying as she had lived, impenitent and heartless. On the morrow, the populace came in crowds to collect her ashes, to preserve them as relics. She was regarded as a martyred saint, and her ashes were supposed to be endowed, by Divine grace, with the power of curing all diseases. Popular folly has often canonised persons whose pretensions to sanctity were extremely equivocal; but the disgusting folly of the multitude, in this instance, has never been surpassed.

Before her death, proceedings were instituted against M. de Penautier, treasurer of the province of Languedoc, and Receiver-general for the clergy, who was accused by a lady, named St Laurent, of having poisoned her husband, the late Receiver-general, in order to obtain his appointment. The circumstances of this case were never divulged, and the greatest influence was exerted to prevent it from going to trial. He was known to have been intimate with Sainte Croix and Mme de Brinvilliers, and was thought to have procured his poisons from them. The latter, however, refused to say anything which might implicate him. The enquiry was eventually stifled, after Penautier had been several months in the Bastille.

The Cardinal de Bonzy was accused by the gossips of the day of being an accomplice of Penautier. The Cardinal's estates were burthened with the payment of several heavy annuities; but, about the time that poisoning became so fashionable, all the annuitants died off, one after the other. The Cardinal, in talking of these annuitants, afterwards used to say, 'Thanks to my star, I have outlived them all!' A wit, seeing him and Penautier riding in the same carriage, cried out, in allusion to this expression, 'There go the Cardinal de Bonzy and his star!'

It was now that the mania for poisoning began to take hold of the popular mind. From this time until the year 1682, the prisons of France teemed with persons accused of this crime; and it is very singular, that other offences decreased in a similar proportion. We have already seen the extent to which it was carried in Italy. It was, if possible, surpassed in France. The diabolical ease with which these murders could be effected, by means of these scentless and tasteless poisons, enticed the evil-minded. Jealousy, revenge, avarice, even petty spite, alike resorted to them. Those who would have been deterred, by fear of detection, from using the pistol or the dagger, or even strong doses of poison, which kill at once, employed slow poisons without dread. The corrupt Government of the day, although it could wink at the atrocities of a wealthy and influential courtier, like Penautier, was scandalised to see the crime spreading among the people. Disgrace was, in fact, entailed, in the eyes of Europe, upon the name of Frenchman. Louis XIV, to put a stop to the evil, instituted what was called the Chambre Ardente, or Burning Chamber, with extensive powers, for the trial and punishment of the prisoners.

Two women, especially, made themselves notorious at this time, and were instrumental to the deaths of hundreds of individuals. They both resided in Paris, and were named Lavoisin and Lavigoreux. Like Spars and Tophania, of whom they were imitators, they chiefly sold their poisons to women who wanted to get rid of their husbands; and, in some few instances, to husbands who wanted to get rid of their wives. Their ostensible occupation was that of midwives. They also pretended to be fortune-tellers, and were visited by persons of every class of society. The rich and poor thronged alike to their *mansardes*, to learn the secrets of the future. Their prophecies were principally of death. They foretold to women the approaching dissolution of husbands, and to needy heirs, the end of rich relatives, who had made them, as Byron expresses it, 'wait too, too long already'. They generally took care to be instrumental in fulfilling their own predictions. They used to tell their wretched employers, that some sign of the approaching death would take place in the house, such as the breaking of glass or china; and they paid servants considerable fees to cause a breakage, as if by accident, exactly at the appointed time. Their occupation as midwives made them acquainted with the secrets of many families, which they afterwards turned to dreadful account.

It is not known how long they had carried on this awful trade before they were discovered. Detection finally overtook them at the close of the year 1679. They were both tried, found guilty, and burned alive on the Place de Grève, on the 22nd of February, 1680, after their hands had been bored through with a red-hot iron, and then cut off. Their numerous accomplices in Paris and in the provinces were also discovered and brought to trial. According to some authors, thirty, and to others, fifty of them, chiefly women, were hanged in the principal cities.

Lavoisin kept a list of the visiters who came to her house to purchase poisons. This paper was seized by the police on her arrest, and examined by the tribunals. Among the names were found those of the Marshal de Luxembourg, the Countess de Soissons, and the Duchess de Bouillon. The Marshal seems only to have been guilty of a piece of discreditable folly in visiting a woman of this description, but the popular voice at the time imputed to him something more than folly. The author of the *Memoirs of the Affairs of Europe since the Peace of Utrecht*, says, 'The miserable gang who dealt in poison and prophecy alleged that he had sold himself to the devil, and that a young girl of the name of Dupin had been poisoned by his means. Among other stories, they said he had made a contract with the devil, in order to marry his son to the daughter of the Marquis of Louvois. To this atrocious and absurd accusation the Marshal, who had surrendered himself at the Bastille on the first accusation against him, replied with the mingled sentiment of pride and innocence, "When Mathieu de Montmorenci, my ancestor, married the widow of Louis le Gros, he did not have recourse to the devil, but to the States-General, in order to obtain for the minor king the support of the house of Montmorenci." This brave man was imprisoned in a cell six feet and a half long, and his trial, which was interrupted for several weeks, lasted altogether fourteen months. No judgement was pronounced upon him.'

The Countess of Soissons fled to Brussels, rather than undergo the risk of a trial; and was never able to clear herself from the stigma that attached to her, of having made an attempt to poison the Queen of Spain by doses of succession powder. The Duchess of Bouillon was arrested, and tried by the Chambre Ardente. It would appear, however, that she had nothing to do with the slow poisons, but had merely endeavoured to pry into the secrets of futurity, and gratify her curiosity with a sight of the devil. One of the presidents of the Chambre, La Reynie, an ugly little old man, very seriously asked her whether she had really seen the devil; to which the lady replied, looking him full in the face, 'Oh yes! I see him now. He is in the form of a little ugly old man, exceedingly ill-natured, and is dressed in the robes of a counsellor of State.' M. la Reynie prudently refrained from asking any more questions of a lady with so sharp and ready a tongue. The Duchess was imprisoned for several months in the Bastille; and nothing being proved against her, she was released at the intercession of her powerful friends. The severe punishment of criminals of this note might have helped to abate the fever of imitation among the vulgar; their comparative impunity had a contrary tendency. The escape of Penautier, and the wealthy Cardinal de Bonzy his employer, had the most pernicious effect. For two years longer the crime continued to rage, and was not finally suppressed till the stake had blazed, or the noose dangled, for upwards of a hundred individuals.*

* Slow poisoning is a crime which has unhappily been revived in England within the last few years, and which has been carried to an extent sufficient to cast a stain upon the national character. The poisoners have been principally women of the lowest class, and their victims have been their husbands or their children. The motive for the crime has in most instances been the basest that can be imagined, the desire to obtain from burial-clubs to which they subscribed, the premium, or burial-money. A recent enactment, restricting the sale of arsenic and other poisons, will, it is to be hoped, check if it do not extirpate, this abominable crime (1851).

THE STORY OF PENGUIN CLASSICS

Before 1946 ... 'Classics' are mainly the domain of academics and students; readable editions for everyone else are almost unheard of. This all changes when a little-known classicist, E. V. Rieu, presents Penguin founder Allen Lane with the translation of Homer's *Odyssey* that he has been working on in his spare time.

1946 Penguin Classics debuts with *The Odyssey*, which promptly sells three million copies. Suddenly, classics are no longer for the privileged few.

1950s Rieu, now series editor, turns to professional writers for the best modern, readable translations, including Dorothy L. Sayers's *Inferno* and Robert Graves's unexpurgated *Twelve Caesars*.

1960s The Classics are given the distinctive black covers that have remained a constant throughout the life of the series. Rieu retires in 1964, hailing the Penguin Classics list as 'the greatest educative force of the twentieth century.'

1970s A new generation of translators swells the Penguin Classics ranks, introducing readers of English to classics of world literature from more than twenty languages. The list grows to encompass more history, philosophy, science, religion and politics.

1980s The Penguin American Library launches with titles such as *Uncle Tom's Cabin*, and joins forces with Penguin Classics to provide the most comprehensive library of world literature available from any paperback publisher.

1990s The launch of Penguin Audiobooks brings the classics to a listening audience for the first time, and in 1999 the worldwide launch of the Penguin Classics website extends their reach to the global online community.

The 21st Century Penguin Classics are completely redesigned for the first time in nearly twenty years. This world-famous series now consists of more than 1300 titles, making the widest range of the best books ever written available to millions – and constantly redefining what makes a 'classic'.

The Odyssey continues ...

The best books ever written

PENGUIN (🐧) CLASSICS

SINCE 1946

Find out more at www.penguinclassics.com